THE BIG BOOK OF
LEGO®
FACTS

THE BIG BOOK OF
LEGO®
FACTS

Written by
Simon Hugo

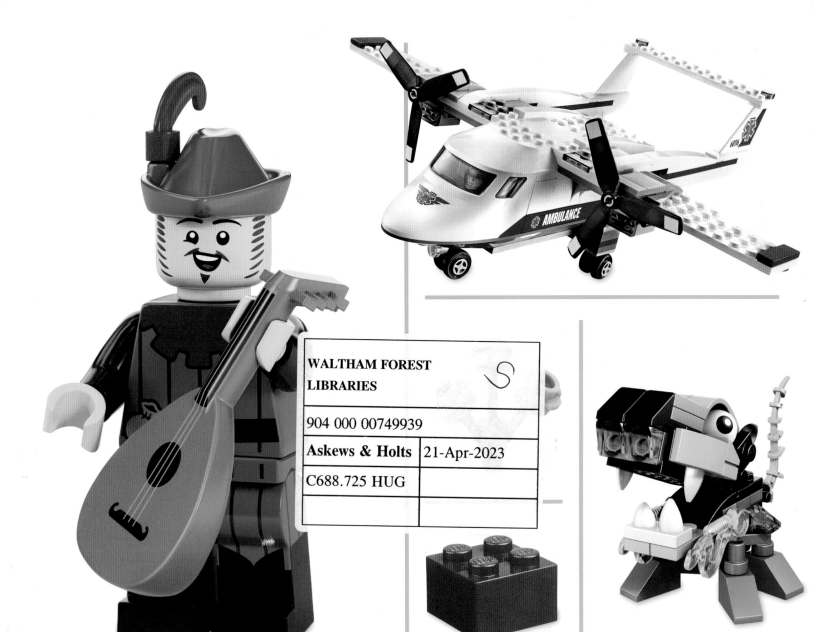

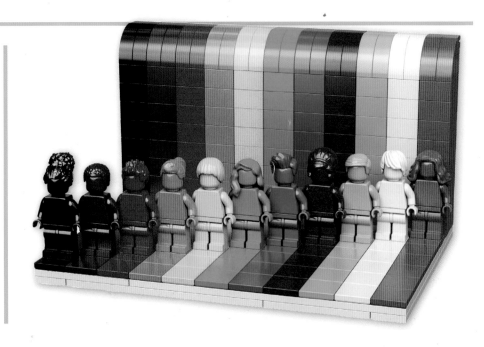

CONTENTS

CHAPTER ONE

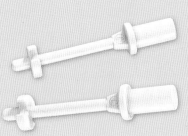

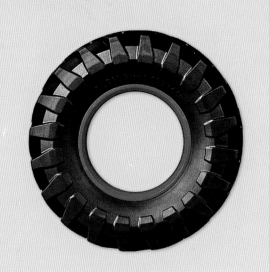

BRICKS AND PIECES

BEFORE THE BRICK

In the years before LEGO® bricks, the business that would become the LEGO Group made other high-quality toys, first from wood, and then from plastic...

WOW!

The wooden LEGO Tractor from 1949 may look basic, but it has functional front-wheel steering, just like a LEGO® Technic set.

FACT STACK

The LEGO Group founder, Ole Kirk Kristiansen, crafted his first wooden toys in 1932.

The first playthings to be sold bearing the LEGO brand name were produced in 1934.

The LEGO Group made its first plastic toys in 1947, alongside its range of wooden items.

REALLY?!

When a craze for wooden yo-yos ended, the LEGO Group turned its leftover stock into colourful wheels for other toys!

Q | Are there any wooden LEGO bricks?

A | No – but there were wooden LEGO blocks. From 1946, stackable cubes were made for early learners. They were painted with brightly coloured letters and numbers.

FUN 5

Pull-along wooden LEGO toys

1 **Duck** opens and closes its beak.

2 **Clumsy Hans** bobs up and down.

3 **Monkey** rocks back and forth.

4 **Dog** turns its head and wags its tail.

5 **Chickens** peck the ground in turn.

AWESOME!

One of the first sets to feature plastic playing pieces, Monypoli was a 1948 board game with squares that spelled out the word "LEGO".

28

wooden toys were listed in Ole Kirk Kristiansen's first product catalogue in 1932, including a fire truck, a racing car, and an aeroplane.

Brick History

One of the most popular early LEGO toys, 1935's wooden LEGO Duck was recreated as a modern, brick-built LEGO set in 2020 and sold exclusively at the LEGO® House visitor attraction in Billund, Denmark.

PLASTIC PLAYTIME

Some of the first plastic LEGO toys included a baby's rattle shaped like a fish and a sailor figure that could slide down a rope.

As a mark of quality and authenticity, most wooden LEGO toys were labelled with a sticker showing an early LEGO logo and proudly proclaiming: "BILLUND DENMARK".

SANDBOX GAME

The first LEGO construction toy was Kirk's Kuglebane ("Kirk's Ball Track", also known as "Kirk's Sand Game"). Released in 1935, it comprised small wooden blocks that could be arranged in a sandbox to make a track for a metal ball.

GET WITH THE SYSTEM

Conceived in 1955, the simple but innovative idea that every plastic LEGO® element should be part of a wider "System" is still at the heart of LEGO building today.

Brick History

In 1954, Godtfred Kirk Christiansen came up with the idea for the LEGO System in Play when the chief buyer for a major Danish department store complained that the toy industry had "no system of any kind"!

FACT STACK

Since 1955, the majority of LEGO sets have been part of the LEGO System in Play.

The LEGO System in Play means that LEGO sets never become obsolete.

The LEGO System in Play is divided into different "themes" such as LEGO® City and LEGO® Friends, which are all compatible.

WOW!

Lots of prototype pieces were made to perfect the "clutch power" that fastens LEGO bricks together without making them too hard to pull apart.

KEY DATES

1949
The company's first plastic bricks are sold as "Automatic Binding Bricks". They have studs on top, but no tubes underneath, and slits on two sides.

1953
Automatic Binding Bricks are officially renamed "LEGO Bricks" ("LEGO Mursten" in Danish). The LEGO name is moulded onto each stud for the first time.

1955
The LEGO System in Play launches with the LEGO Town Plan: 28 LEGO brick-building sets plus eight vehicles, all designed to be used together.

1957
Tubes are built into the underside of LEGO bricks so that they clutch securely to the studs on top of the one below. The new bricks go on sale in 1958.

1958
Stud-and-tube interlocking is one of several brick-building systems covered by the LEGO brick patent, awarded on January 28.

915,103,765

The number of ways that six classic 2×4 LEGO bricks of the same colour can be combined.

AWESOME!
Today's 2×4 LEGO bricks have exactly the same measurements as the ones made in the 1950s. They will fit perfectly with any brick from the past 60 years.

1

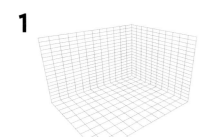

Design grid

2

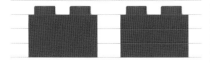

1 brick = 3 plates

3

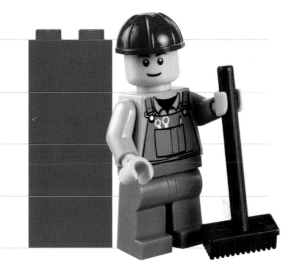

1 minifigure stands 4 bricks high

ON THE GRID

1 To ensure all elements fit in the LEGO System in Play, new LEGO parts are designed according to a three-dimensional grid.

2 Making sure all LEGO elements align within the grid increases the potential for parts to serve more than one function – in future sets or simply in creative play.

3 Even specialized pieces such as minifigures and accessories must conform to the grid. This ensures they can connect with other pieces in as many ways as possible.

REALLY?!

They may not look like it at first, but even curvy, organic-looking parts are designed to fit the LEGO System in Play.

Q What are LEGO bricks made from?

A Early LEGO bricks were made from cellulose acetate. Since 1963, they have mostly been made from a more durable plastic called acrylonitrile butadiene styrene (ABS). Today, various special elements are also made from sustainably sourced plant-based plastic called biopolyethylene.

WOW!

Amazingly, there are 24 different ways to combine just two 2×4 LEGO bricks. See if you can manage to find them all!

MAKING PLANS

Before LEGO "themes" as we know them today, Town Plan sets were the first LEGO products to combine small, brick-built models into an ever-growing urban scene.

Piece particulars

Some LEGO elements are named after the designer that made them. The Erling brick is one of them, named after LEGO designer Erling Dideriksen who invented this element in 1979.

THE SPECIALS

Since the early days of LEGO® building, there have been special elements to help you build in different ways – and many of the most useful are still around today! Here are 25 bricks and pieces that really put the fun in fundamentals...

Start here! ——

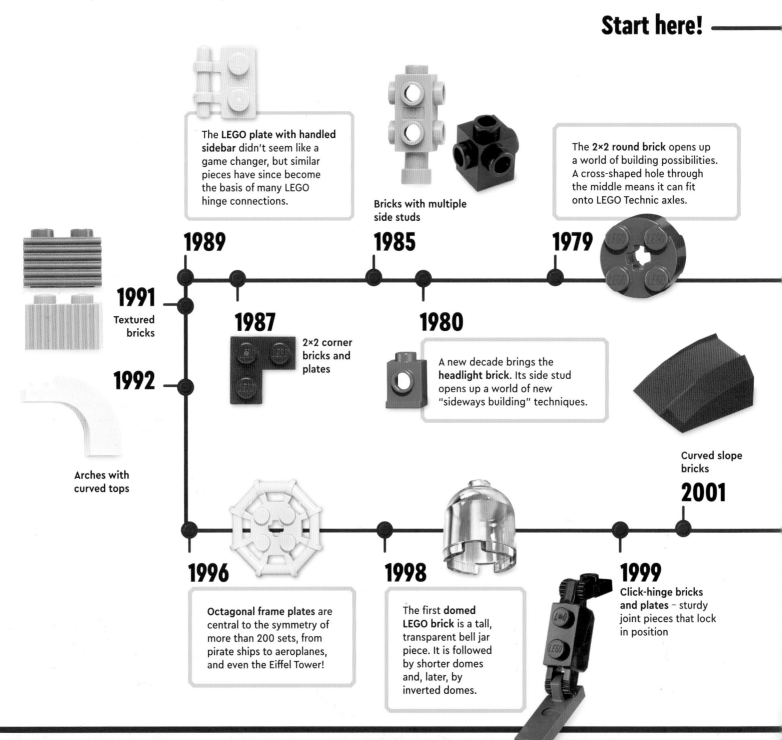

The **LEGO plate with handled sidebar** didn't seem like a game changer, but similar pieces have since become the basis of many LEGO hinge connections.

Bricks with multiple side studs

The **2×2 round brick** opens up a world of building possibilities. A cross-shaped hole through the middle means it can fit onto LEGO Technic axles.

1989

1985

1979

1991

Textured bricks

1987

2×2 corner bricks and plates

1980

A new decade brings the **headlight brick**. Its side stud opens up a world of new "sideways building" techniques.

1992

Arches with curved tops

Curved slope bricks

2001

1996

Octagonal frame plates are central to the symmetry of more than 200 sets, from pirate ships to aeroplanes, and even the Eiffel Tower!

1998

The first **domed LEGO brick** is a tall, transparent bell jar piece. It is followed by shorter domes and, later, by inverted domes.

1999

Click-hinge bricks and plates – sturdy joint pieces that lock in position

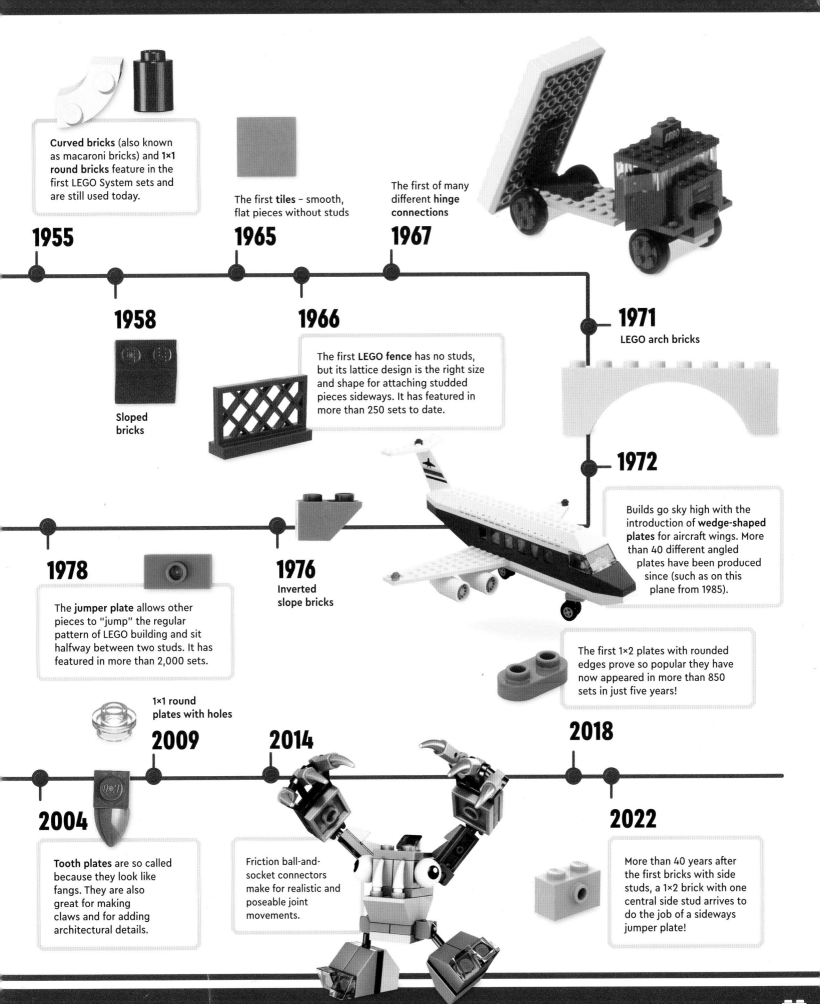

Curved bricks (also known as macaroni bricks) and 1×1 round bricks feature in the first LEGO System sets and are still used today.

1955

The first tiles – smooth, flat pieces without studs

1965

The first of many different hinge connections

1967

1958

Sloped bricks

1966

The first LEGO fence has no studs, but its lattice design is the right size and shape for attaching studded pieces sideways. It has featured in more than 250 sets to date.

1971

LEGO arch bricks

1972

Builds go sky high with the introduction of wedge-shaped plates for aircraft wings. More than 40 different angled plates have been produced since (such as on this plane from 1985).

1978

The jumper plate allows other pieces to "jump" the regular pattern of LEGO building and sit halfway between two studs. It has featured in more than 2,000 sets.

1976

Inverted slope bricks

The first 1×2 plates with rounded edges prove so popular they have now appeared in more than 850 sets in just five years!

1×1 round plates with holes

2009

2014

2018

2004

Tooth plates are so called because they look like fangs. They are also great for making claws and for adding architectural details.

Friction ball-and-socket connectors make for realistic and poseable joint movements.

2022

More than 40 years after the first bricks with side studs, a 1×2 brick with one central side stud arrives to do the job of a sideways jumper plate!

TALLEST TYRE

The tyres introduced for the LEGO Technic CLAAS XERION 5000 TRAC VC tractor (set 42054) in 2016 stand a whopping 107 mm (4 in) high!

REINVENTING THE WHEEL

One good turn deserves another, and there's always a new LEGO® wheel rolling into view! Here are the top tyres and weirdest wheels...

AWESOME! The most wheels on an individual vehicle (so not including trains and trucks with trailers) is 14, on the LEGO City Cargo Plane (set 7734) from 2008.

FUN 5

Wheels that make the LEGO world go round

1 Steering wheel (1978)

2 Cartwheel (1984)

3 Ship's wheel (1985)

4 Fancy carriage wheel (2014)

5 Wheelchair wheel (2016)

HEAVIEST TYRE

The heaviest LEGO tyres were made for the LEGO Technic Power Puller (set 8457). Each 170 g (6 oz) tyre weighs more than 150 standard LEGO City car tyres.

Piece particulars

The LEGO Fabuland Paddle Steamer (set 3673) from 1985 is the only set to feature a waterwheel piece. It is also the first set to use the ship's steering wheel piece!

REALLY?!

LEGO City Tyre Escape (set 60126) features one large tyre but no wheels. The tyre is used as a boat by an escaping crook!

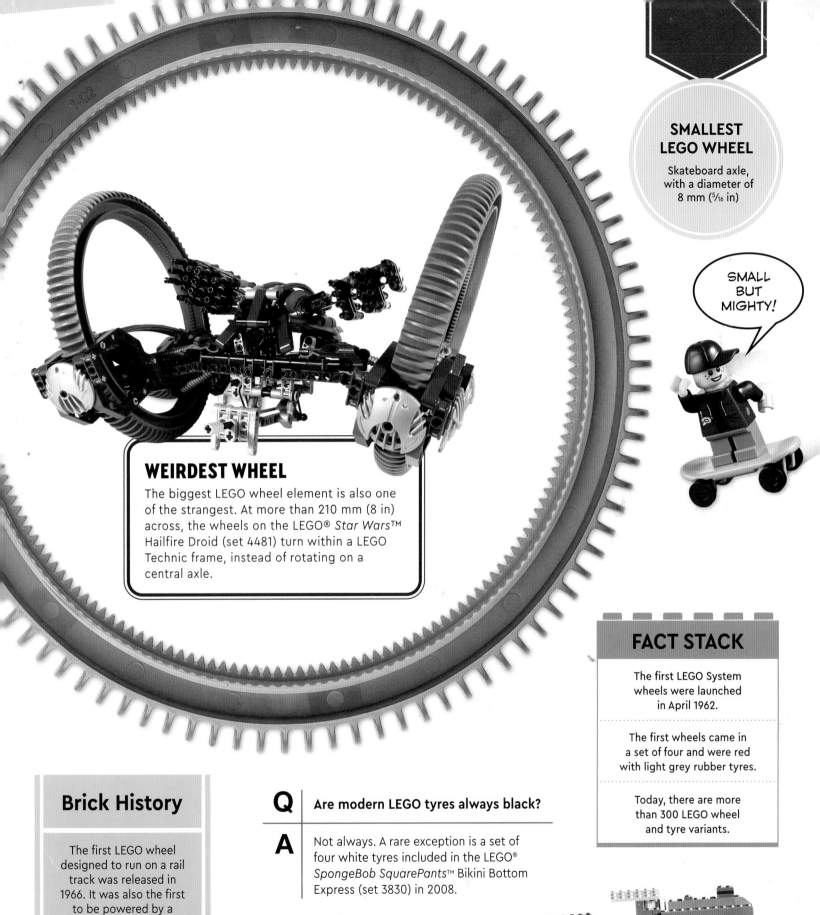

SMALL
BUT
MIGHTY!

WEIRDEST WHEEL

The biggest LEGO wheel element is also one
of the strangest. At more than 210 mm (8 in)
across, the wheels on the LEGO® *Star Wars*™
Hailfire Droid (set 4481) turn within a LEGO
Technic frame, instead of rotating on a
central axle.

FACT STACK

The first LEGO System
wheels were launched
in April 1962.

The first wheels came in
a set of four and were red
with light grey rubber tyres.

Today, there are more
than 300 LEGO wheel
and tyre variants.

Brick History

The first LEGO wheel
designed to run on a rail
track was released in
1966. It was also the first
to be powered by a
motor in Motorized Train
Set (set 113).

Q | Are modern LEGO tyres always black?

A | Not always. A rare exception is a set of
four white tyres included in the LEGO®
SpongeBob SquarePants™ Bikini Bottom
Express (set 3830) in 2008.

POST   POST   HAMBURG BASEL GENOVA

THE LEGO® COLOUR CHART

CLASSIC COLOURS

These six classic colours have been used in LEGO® sets for more than 50 years.

Bright Red

Bright Yellow

White

Dark Green
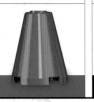

Bright Blue

Black

Cool Yellow
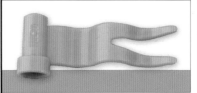

Bright Orange
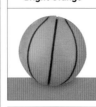

Flame Yellowish Orange

Bright Purple

Light Purple

Bright Red Violet

Vibrant Yellow

Light Royal Blue
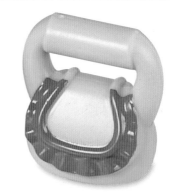

Vibrant Coral
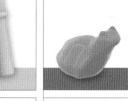

Medium Blue

Sand Blue

Earth Blue
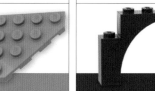

Sand Green
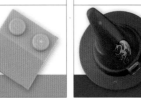

Earth Green

Spring Yellowish Green

Bright Yellow Green

Olive Green

Reddish Brown

Nougat

Light Nougat

Dark Orange

Medium Stone Grey

Transparent Yellow

Transparent Bright Orange

Transparent Fluorescent Red Orange

Transparent Red

Transparent Medium Violet

Transparent Bright Violet

Transparent Blue

Transparent Light Blue

LEGO elements have been made in more than 150 shades since the 1950s. This rainbow of colour covers hues that have recently been in production.

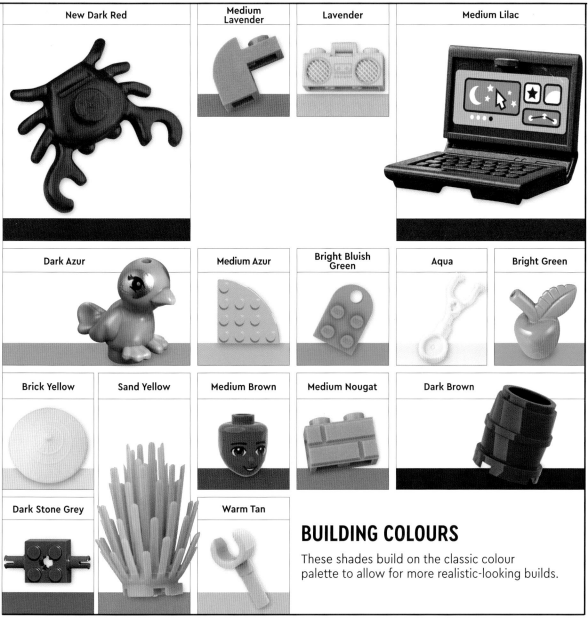

New Dark Red	Medium Lavender	Lavender	Medium Lilac

Dark Azur	Medium Azur	Bright Bluish Green	Aqua	Bright Green

Brick Yellow	Sand Yellow	Medium Brown	Medium Nougat	Dark Brown

Dark Stone Grey		Warm Tan		

BUILDING COLOURS

These shades build on the classic colour palette to allow for more realistic-looking builds.

SPECIAL COLOURS

Starting with metallic colours in the 1970s, this range now also includes glittery, opalescent, and glow-in-the-dark elements.

Titanium Metallic

Warm Gold	White Glow

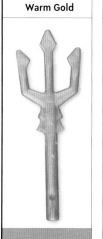 

Silver Metallic

Silver Glitter (added to transparent colours)	Transparent Opalescent (comes in various shades)

Transparent Green	Transparent Fluorescent Green	Transparent Bright Green	Transparent Brown	Transparent Black	Transparent

TRANSPARENT COLOURS

Transparent tones joined the LEGO colour palette in the late 1960s.

THE PATH TO POWER

Lots of electrical innovations have brought light, sound, and movement to LEGO® sets over the years, culminating in today's "Powered Up" sets.

Start here! —

New "Code Pilot" technology emerges in **LEGO Technic Barcode Multi-Set** (set 8479). Scanning special barcodes controls the speed, sound, and actions of this motorized tipper truck.

The first **LEGO® MINDSTORMS® sets** use infrared technology to send instructions from your computer to "smart bricks" built into a range of robots.

1998

1998

With instructions for building five powered cars, **Radio Control Racer** (set 5600) is the first set to come with a wireless remote-control unit.

The LEGO® Studios theme launches with a **digital camera** built like a large LEGO element. The camera can be fixed into place for making stop-motion LEGO movies.

1997

The LEGO® Space UFO **Interstellar Starfighter** (set 6979) is one of the only sets to feature fibre–optic cables, which light up with an eerie alien glow.

The compact **LEGO Technic Speed Computer** (set 5206) appears, allowing you to measure the speed, travel time, and distance covered by your vehicle builds.

2000

2002

Send any **LEGO® Spybotics** set on an undercover mission and it will follow your programmed instructions, using light and touch sensors to find its way.

Electric light comes to LEGO sets with the first **light-up brick**. A replaceable bulb inside the transparent 2×4 brick connects to a 4.5-volt battery.

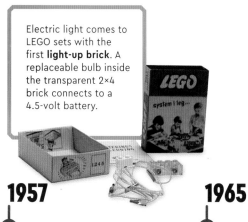

1957

The first **battery-powered LEGO motor** is launched in North America. Wheels attach directly to the transparent "Motor Pak", which has studs on top for building.

1965

New 4.5-volt motors herald the arrival of **powered LEGO trains**. The motors can also be fitted with tyres instead of train wheels for building motorized cars.

1966

The **LEGO® Light and Sound System** adds working sirens and flashing LED lights to Town and Space sets, powered by the first 9-volt LEGO battery boxes.

1977

The first **LEGO Technic sets** are released with instructions on how to motorize them using the more compact 4.5-volt motor designed for this theme.

The **LEGO Technic Control Centre** (set 8094) offers the power to build four programmable machines, including a robot arm and a drawing device.

1990

1986

The first sound bricks with built-in batteries add va-va-VROOOM to eight different motorbike builds in **LEGO® Creator Revvin' Riders** (set 4893).

The dawn of **LEGO Power Functions** marks the start of a whole new era of battery-operated functionality in 21st-century LEGO sets.

2006

2007

2003

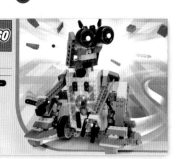

A new, unique memory module in **LEGO Creator Record and Play** (set 4095) remembers how you moved a model, and then replays those movements!

2018

The **LEGO Powered Up** platform unites motorized sets across a range of themes, with new smart components and a dedicated app.

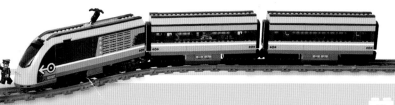

THE ELECTRIC COMPANY

Since 2018, the LEGO Group has used Powered Up motors and app-controlled elements to bring sets to life like never before!

Brick statistics

LEGO® Ideas Grand Piano (set 21323)

3,662 pieces
Including a well-hidden Powered Up Hub

562 pages
Make up the massive building instructions book

25 keys
That move as the app-controlled music plays

10 built-in tunes
Including "Happy Birthday to You" and "Jingle Bells"

36 cm (14 in)
From front to back, and 23 cm (9 in) tall

FACT STACK

The Powered Up platform combines smart hubs, motors, sensors, and lights with standard LEGO parts.

Powered Up builds are controlled wirelessly, usually with an app on a smartphone or tablet.

Besides Powered Up motors, electrical components in LEGO sets include working lights and sound bricks.

7
motors power the enormous LEGO Technic Liebherr R 9800 excavator, making it move on mighty caterpillar tracks and dig for LEGO bricks!

Piece particulars

Each Powered Up LEGO City train comes with a 10-speed Bluetooth remote control. This can be used to drive the train without a smartphone or tablet.

REALLY?!

Drive the LEGO Technic App-Controlled Transformation Vehicle (set 42140) into a wall, and it will flip over and reverse away on its "back"!

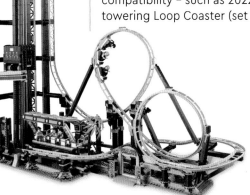

Q **Can Powered Up parts be added to any LEGO set?**

A Anything's possible with a little imagination! But some sets are specially designed for Powered Up compatibility – such as 2022's towering Loop Coaster (set 10303).

FUN 5

Non-motorized sets with working lights

1 Spring Lantern Festival (set 80107)

2 Gingerbread House (set 10267)

3 Haunted House (set 10273)

4 Robo Explorer (set 31062)

5 Lighthouse Point (set 31051)

Brick History

The first Powered Up set was the LEGO® DC Super Heroes App-Controlled Batmobile (set 76112) in 2018, complete with an exclusive Batman minifigure.

I'M APP-MAN!

AWESOME!

LEGO Powered Up components are fully compatible with LEGO® Boost coding sets, sets such as 2019's LEGO *Star Wars* Droid Commander (set 75253), with its working R2-D2!

Plants and flowers of the LEGO® world

1 **Trees and Bushes (set 230)**
Rare; these early bloomers were designed to add greenery to the LEGO Town Plan theme of the 1950s, but could not be built onto other elements. In the mid 1960s, LEGO trees were redesigned with bases that could be built onto other elements, but retained their detailed, real-world look.

2 **Fruit tree from Trees and Signs (set 990)**
Rare; most LEGO elements are made from tiny granules of plastic that are heated and shaped in a mould. For this 1970s LEGO tree, those granules were only partially melted to create a leafy look.

3 **Flowers**
Widespread; the most abundant and diverse flora in the LEGO biosphere, LEGO flowers bloom most commonly in red, but also in blue, yellow, white, and four shades of pink.

4 **Cypress tree**
Rare; dating back to the time of the first LEGO® Castle sets, this tree was found in just a handful of sets in the 1980s.

BOTANY

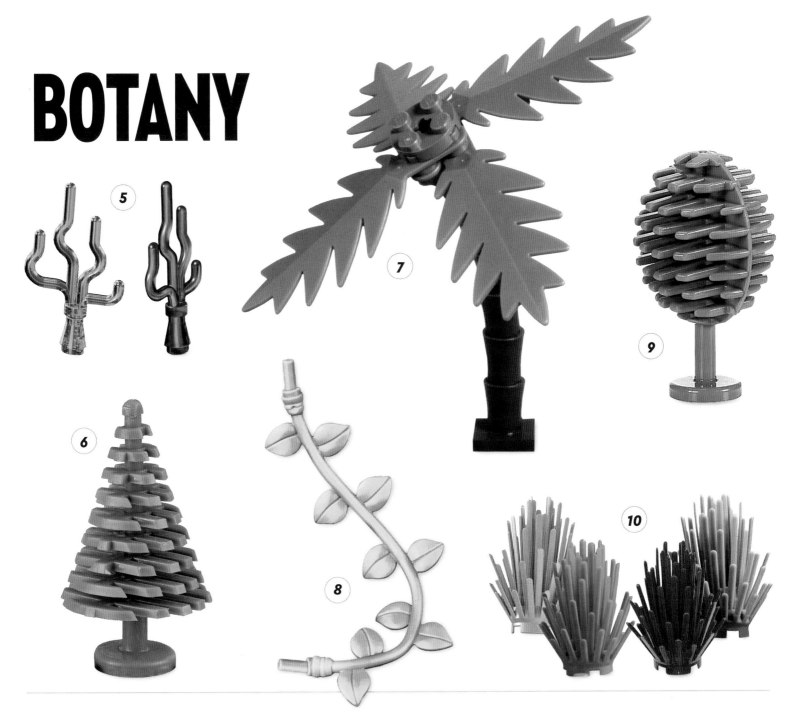

5 **Seagrass**
Widespread; frequently found in underwater habitats, but also seen on mountains, in parks, and on islands.

6 **Pine tree**
Widespread; the most common LEGO tree has appeared in more than 150 sets since 1971. A smaller pine has also been widely cultivated since 1986.

7 **Palm tree**
Widespread; originally limited to tropical areas frequented by LEGO® Pirates, a variety with shorter leaves (pictured) has since been found in Heartlake City, home of LEGO Friends.

8 **Leafy vine**
Restricted; recently discovered by LEGO botanists, this flexible vine has become established in Heartlake City.

9 **Fruit tree**
Relict; once a familiar sight in LEGO Town and LEGO City, this fruit tree was last seen in 2010. A scarce lime variety was found in one Creator set in 2013.

10 **Prickly bush**
Widespread; this adaptable shrub has been noted in more than 140 locations, mostly in green but also in tan, dark tan, and red.

KEY DATES

1977
Also known as Expert Builder Sets, the first Technical Set models include a forklift truck, a tractor, and a helicopter.

1984
The LEGO Technic theme name appears on boxes for the first time, and the first pneumatic sets use compressed air pumps to power machine functions.

1990
The battery-powered Control Centre (set 8094) brings basic programming functionality to LEGO Technic sets for the first time.

1999
A forerunner of LEGO® BIONICLE®, the LEGO Technic Slizer subtheme (known as Throwbots in North America) stars disc-throwing alien robots!

2007
Remote-controlled Power Functions add new electronic features to larger LEGO Technic sets. Motorized Bulldozer (set 8275) was the first, and won the Nuremberg Innovation Award.

2017
Building instructions for a new model based on 1980's Car Chassis (set 8860) are part of the celebrations for LEGO Technic's 40th anniversary.

Q Why do most LEGO Technic beams have an odd number of holes when most LEGO bricks have an even number of studs?

A Because any beam with an odd number of holes will always have a connecting point right in the middle – and combining two such beams still allows for even-numbered lengths.

Brick History

In 1996, the first LEGO Technic studless beam appeared in Space Shuttle (set 8480). Today, studless beams have largely replaced brick-style beams in LEGO Technic sets.

LOOK CLOSER

Not all LEGO Technic pins are created equal! Black, blue, and red pins have extra ridges so that they make a tighter connection than grey, tan, and white-coloured ones.

AWESOME!
More than 30 LEGO Technic sets come with pullback motors so they can speed into action without needing batteries.

Brick statistics

100+ LEGO Technic cars
From go-karts to F1 racers

65+ construction vehicles
Diggers, cranes, dozers, and more

55+ trucks and tractors
2021's Heavy-Duty Tow Truck (set 42128, pictured)

40+ motorcycles
Including trikes and ATVs

35+ aeroplanes and helicopters
Plus a single Space Shuttle

FACT STACK

The first LEGO gears came out in 1965. They are not compatible with LEGO Technic elements.

There are more than 20 types of LEGO Technic gears, counting rack and pinion elements.

Today, many large LEGO System sets are built around a sturdy core of LEGO Technic parts.

FUN 5

Essential LEGO Technic elements

1 **Beams** form the "skeleton" of any LEGO Technic vehicle.

2 **Pins** connect beams and other parts at any angle.

3 **Axles** slot through beams to connect moving parts.

4 **Gears** are wheels with teeth that turn on axles.

5 **Bushes** space out elements and hold axles in place.

40 teeth on the largest LEGO Technic gearwheel.

Piece particulars

Flexible rod parts added cool curves and extra functionality to LEGO Technic sets in 1991. Today, flexible cross axles and cable parts still form part of the theme's aesthetic.

LET'S GET TECHNICAL

Over the past 45 years, budding engineers have been using LEGO® Technic elements to build bigger, more complex models full of moving parts and working mechanisms.

IT'S A SIGN! Every LEGO Technic set released in 2017 came with a special printed beam celebrating the theme's 40th anniversary.

LEGO® HOMEMAKING

Doors

1

2

3

4

Windows

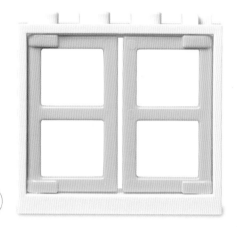

1

2

3

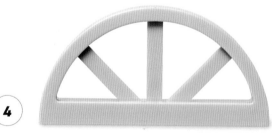

4

1 This **door with four panes** was introduced alongside the first minifigures in 1978. A similar design set into a frame was introduced in 2008.

2 Few LEGO homes in the 1980s were complete without a stylish **door with six panes**! Left- and right-handed versions were made in five colours.

3 For a more rustic look, you can't beat an **arched door** with a lattice window. First seen in 2001, the design was updated with new hinges in 2010.

4 The first dedicated **corner door** frame arrived in sets in 2017. Dozens of different doors can be set into the frame, opening to the left or right.

1 With its opening panes and optional shutters, this **casement window** from 1978 can also be fitted with a single clear pane.

3 Seen in more than 180 sets since 1996, this **arched window** frame can be fitted with two kinds of lattice, or left completely clear.

2 For a modern look, build your LEGO house with plain **window panel** pieces, produced in various shapes, sizes, and colours since 1982.

4 This 2015 **fanlight** piece is designed to let light in above a LEGO door, and fits snugly inside the curve of a modern 1×6×2 arch brick.

Fences

1 This classic **lattice fence** design has been seen outside LEGO houses since 1967 – long before there were minifigures to live inside them!

2 Two types of **railings** have appeared in around 300 sets since 1996. End to end, they would stretch more than 300 m (990 ft)!

3 Since 2000, **white picket fences** have appeared in more than 70 sets in gleaming white. It's a brave minifigure who erects the (much rarer) bright yellow ones!

4 This **ornamental fence** brought a Bohemian twist to LEGO builds in 2015. A more angular ornamental design followed in 2017.

Interiors

1 The classic minifigure **chair** was introduced in 1980. It has since made itself comfortable in more than 1,000 sets!

3 Designed to be fitted with an opening cupboard door or drawers, this stylish **storage unit** has been around since 1985.

2 Introduced as a mailbox in 1982, this opening element is now often used by minifigures and mini dolls as a **freezer** or an **oven**.

4 Since 2011, minifigures in more than 50 sets have added bling to their bathrooms and kitchens using this pearl gold **mixer tap**!

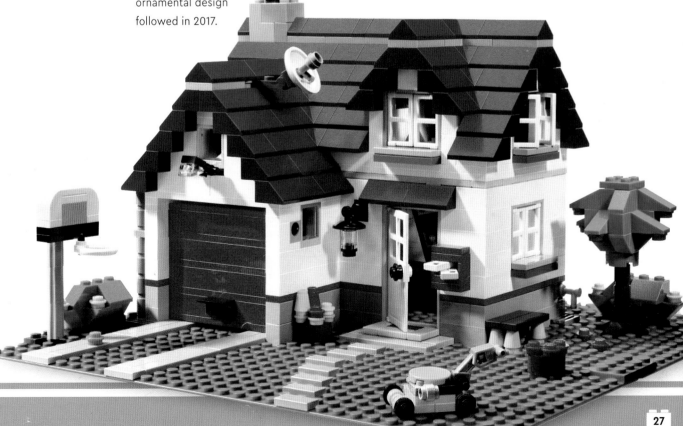

PLENTY OF PIECES

With LEGO® sets coming in all shapes and sizes – from tall and thin to wide and flat – it can be hard to know which is the biggest. But these 10 sets are the largest ever in terms of the number of pieces it takes to build them!

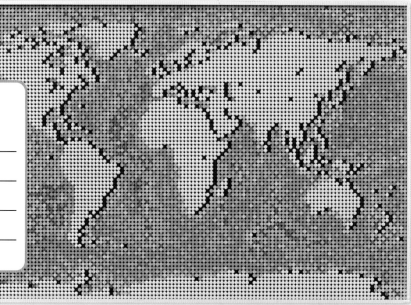

1

11,695 PIECES
WORLD MAP

SET NUMBER	31203
YEAR RELEASED	2021
HEIGHT	66 cm (26 in)
WIDTH	104 cm (41 in)

2

9,090 PIECES
TITANIC

SET NUMBER	10294
YEAR RELEASED	2021
HEIGHT	44 cm (17 in)
LENGTH	135 cm (53 in)

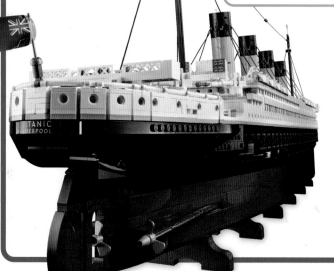

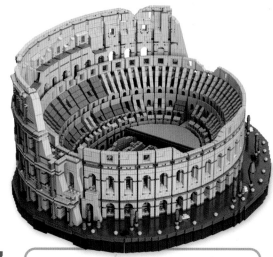

3

9,036 PIECES
COLOSSEUM

SET NUMBER	10276
YEAR RELEASED	2020
HEIGHT	27 cm (11 in)
WIDTH	52 cm (20 in)

4

7,541 PIECES
MILLENNIUM FALCON

SET NUMBER	75192
YEAR RELEASED	2017
LENGTH	84 cm (33 in)
WIDTH	56 cm (22 in)

5

6,785 PIECES
AT-AT

SET NUMBER	75313
YEAR RELEASED	2021
HEIGHT	62 cm (24 in)
LENGTH	69 cm (27 in)

6

6,020 PIECES
HOGWARTS CASTLE

SET NUMBER	71043
YEAR RELEASED	2018
HEIGHT	58 cm (22 in)
WIDTH	69 cm (27 in)

7

5,922 PIECES
TAJ MAHAL

SET NUMBER	10189/10256
YEAR RELEASED	2008/2017
HEIGHT	43 cm (17 in)
WIDTH	51 cm (20 in)

8

5,876 PIECES
REAL MADRID SANTIAGO BERNABÉU STADIUM

SET NUMBER	10299
YEAR RELEASED	2022
HEIGHT	38 cm (15 in)
WIDTH	44 cm (17 in)

9

5,685 PIECES
LEGO® NINJAGO® CITY GARDENS

SET NUMBER	71741
YEAR RELEASED	2021
HEIGHT	73 cm (29 in)
WIDTH	44 cm (17 in)

10

5,544 PIECES
DIAGON ALLEY

SET NUMBER	75978
YEAR RELEASED	2020
HEIGHT	29 cm (11 in)
WIDTH	102 cm (40 in)

Some of the most intricate and adorable LEGO® parts are the everyday objects made to be held in minifigure hands...

ASSORTED

Fun and games

1   Minifigures have cared for cuddly toys such as this **teddy bear** since 2012. More recently, a bunny has bounced into sets as well.

2   The most magical thing about the **balloon animals** made by 2018's Party Clown Minifigure is that they never, ever burst!

Sports

3   **Ski poles** are most commonly found in white, but they were also made in pearl gold to top the turrets of the LEGO Big Ben (set 21013) in 2016.

4   The removable weights of this **barbell** are used by minifigures in training, but can also serve as hubcaps on LEGO cars!

Music

5   Minifigure musical instruments include guitars, saxophones, maracas, and even this Troubadour's medieval **lute**!

6   **Portable stereos** have appeared in lots of sets since 2011, but 2020's Fitness Instructor was the first to enjoy her tunes in toe-tapping turquoise!

Tools of the trade

7   The **paint roller** piece fits on to any 1×1 round brick to change the paint colour. It first appeared with a light blue sleeve in 2013.

8   More than 400 minifigures have set to work with a **shovel** since 1978, but only the Dog Sitter carries one in bright green – ideal for scooping poop!

ACCESSORIES

Ways of seeing

9 The transparent lens of a LEGO **magnifying glass** really works, enhancing the sight of minifigures and LEGO builders alike!

10 Though **binoculars** appear in more than 500 sets, only the Lifeguard Minifigure gets a bright red pair to match his rescue buoy.

Gadgets

11 The Video Games Champ was the first to get to grips with this **games controller** piece in 2019. A different design is found in LEGO NINJAGO sets.

12 **Camera** pieces capture minifigure memories in more than 200 sets. A 1×1 round brick fixed to the front makes an impressive zoom lens!

Reading matter

13 From the *Daily Brick* to the *Zombie Times*, there's a **newspaper** for every minifigure – always printed on a smooth tile piece.

14 The parts used to make minifigure **books** since 2016 also feature in sets as laptop computers, so they always open up a world of knowledge.

Food and drink

15 A single element representing two **chopsticks** was introduced in 2022. It is often paired with a minifigure bowl piece.

16 Minifigures drink from **mugs** in more than 750 sets. They have been made in more than 20 thirst-quenching colours since 1979!

NICE PART USE

Finding a familiar piece and then using it in an unexpected way is called nice part use, or "NPU", by many LEGO® fans. These NPUs prove there is never just one use for any LEGO element!

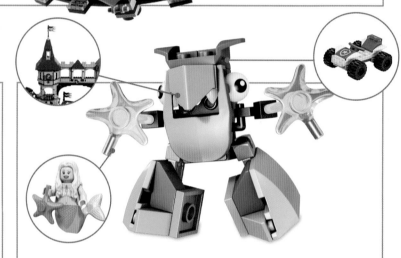

The Alien Mothership (set 7065) from 2011's LEGO® Space Alien Conquest theme uses eight pieces of **railway track** to create its saucer shape.

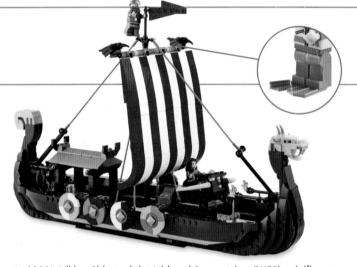

In 2022's Viking Ship and the Midgard Serpent (set 31132), minifigure diving flippers are used to make both the serpent's gills and two pairs of birds' wings.

Torts (set 41520) from 2014's LEGO® Mixels™ range has **starfish** for hands, a **roof piece** for a nose, and **wheel arches** for eyebrows.

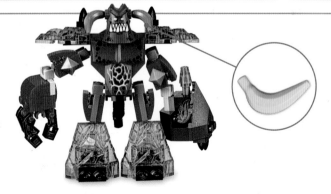

Some fairly bruised-looking **banana pieces** make horns for Burnzie the Lava Monster in the 2016 LEGO® NEXO KNIGHTS™ set Axl's Tower Carrier (set 70322).

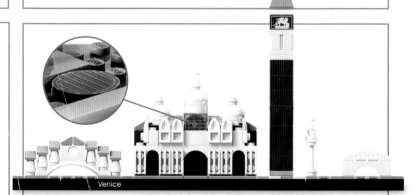

In 2016's LEGO® Architecture Skyline of Venice (set 21026), a printed round tile more often used as an **air vent** becomes the huge, semi-circular window of St Mark's Basilica.

Designed for LEGO *Star Wars* sets, two droid legs form part of a dragon's face in Jay's Cyber Dragon (set 71711), from 2020's LEGO NINJAGO range.

Among the many ingeniously designed lavatories in LEGO sets is one made from a clamshell in 2020's LEGO Friends Beach House (set 41428)!

Take a close look at 2021's LEGO Botanical Collection Bird of Paradise (set 10289) and you'll see three minifigure swords amid the blooms!

This 2021 Police Station (set 10278) includes bushes made out of curved cogwheel pieces and roof details made out of LEGO® Minecraft® creature heads!

CHAPTER TWO

BUILDING
WORLDS

STARTING BRICKS

LEGO® DUPLO® is a world of bigger bricks for smaller hands. Since 1969, it has inspired generations of preschoolers to learn more about the world around them through colourful, creative play.

WOW!

The name DUPLO comes from the Latin word for "double". That's because LEGO DUPLO bricks are double the height, length, and width of standard LEGO bricks!

FACT STACK

LEGO DUPLO debuted in Europe in 1969 and in the US in 1973.

In the US, the LEGO DUPLO theme was known as "Pre-School" until 1979.

The first LEGO DUPLO set was made up of just nine LEGO DUPLO bricks in four colours.

IT'S A SIGN!

duplo

The friendly LEGO DUPLO rabbit logo was launched in 1979 and is now cuter than ever! In 1985, there was a soft and cuddly version that you could store your bricks inside!

REALLY?!

The first ever LEGO toilet appeared in Bathroom (set 2754) in 1986. It was bright green!

AWESOME!

Some LEGO DUPLO toys are designed especially to be used in the bath – like the friendly flamingo in 2022's Bath Time Fun: Floating Animal Island (set 10966)!

KEY DATES

1977
The first LEGO DUPLO people have block-shaped bodies with no arms or legs, and heads that turn but don't come off.

1980
A grey horse in Car and Horse Box (set 2627) is the first of many moulded LEGO DUPLO animals.

1983
The first articulated LEGO DUPLO characters are more like LEGO minifigures, only larger, with realistic flesh tones and no detachable parts.

2004
LEGO DUPLO figures first seen in LEGO® Education sets arrive in stores, looking more realistic than ever, with adorable moulded noses!

9,876,543,210
The biggest number you can make with 2021's Number Train – Learn to Count (set 10954)!

Piece particulars
Since 2019, several LEGO DUPLO sets have included special sound bricks. They range from sirens in fire engine sets to realistic animal sounds. The cute characters in My First Puppy & Kitten with Sounds (set 10977) even snore when they're "asleep"!

Q When did the LEGO DUPLO Zoo close?

A The Zoo theme was a firm favourite from 1990, but LEGO DUPLO animals have been released into the wild since 2009. They now appear in sets based on their natural environments, such as the Savannah, the Arctic, and the Jungle.

Brick History

The first four LEGO DUPLO sets included a handful of standard 2×4 LEGO bricks to demonstrate their compatibility with the much larger LEGO DUPLO bricks.

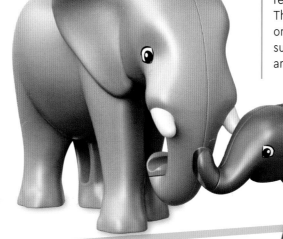

THE SIGHTS OF LEGO® CITY

There's lots to see and do in LEGO® City! Use this visitor's guide to get the most out of your stay, but remember that the street plan is subject to change – a lot!

TRAIN STATION

The bright and modern Train Station (set 60335) is your gateway to the City. Pick up a croissant in the café before hopping on the number 43 bus.

USEFUL INFORMATION

GETTING AROUND
LEGO City is well served by buses, trams, trains, planes, and ferries, as well as new blue cycle lanes.

DINING
There are endless dining options in LEGO City, where even the street vendors are smartly dressed chefs!

ACCOMMODATION
Check out the Capital City Hotel, which opened in 2018, or keep moving with a camper van.

BANKING
Be sure to visit the City Bank before the local crooks arrive with their giant safe-snatching magnet!

FARMERS' MARKET

The LEGO City Farm grows everything from pumpkins to chilli peppers. Pick up some fresh produce during your visit from the Farmers' Market Van (set 60345).

STUNT ARENA

The action-packed Double Loop Stunt Arena (set 60339) is the City's hottest tourist attraction. Just don't get too close to the wall of flames!

SPACEPORT

LEGO City has an extensive space programme, so try to time your visit with a blast-off at the Rocket Launch Centre (set 60351).

TOWN CENTRE

Head for the bustling Town Centre (set 60292) for everything such as fresh pizza, martial arts classes, pocket parks, and electric vehicle charging!

WILDLIFE RESCUE CAMP

The City has plenty of green spaces, but few are as lively as the Wildlife Rescue Camp (set 60307)! Eagles, elephants, lions, and monkeys all roam happily here.

SKI RESORT

Head into the City's mountains for skiing, snowboarding, and year-round snowman building!

SKATE PARK

Everyone is welcome at the City Skate Park (set 60290), where skilled skateboarders rub shoulders with brilliant bikers and wheelchair wizards!

COPS VS. CROOKS

The LEGO City police department keeps crooks at bay and kids at play. Happily, there's no height requirement to join!

REALLY?!

There were no LEGO minifigure crooks in sets until 1993 – and no handcuff pieces to detain them with until 2008!

FACT STACK

There are more than 175 LEGO Town and City police sets.

The first police set was Police Heliport (set 354), released in 1972.

The biggest police set is 2008's Police Headquarters (set 7744), with 953 pieces.

FUN 5

LEGO City Police precincts

1 **City forest**
Forest Police Station (set 4440), 2012

2 **City swamp**
Swamp Police Station (set 60069), 2015

3 **City jail**
Prison Island (set 60130), 2016

4 **City mountains**
Mountain Police Headquarters (set 60174), 2018

5 **City centre**
Police station (set 60316), 2022

▌ AWESOME!
1985's Mobile Police Truck (set 6450) was the first LEGO police vehicle to have flashing lights and a siren. ▌

WOW!

In 2022's Police Chase at the Bank (set 60317), crook Hacksaw Hank tries to make a getaway on a drone loaded with loot!

KEY DATES

1978
The first police minifigure was also the first LEGO minifigure ever. He went on patrol with a stick-on uniform and a police car he couldn't fit into!

1980
The first female LEGO police officer came in a special set for schools. She had white hair that matched her open-topped patrol car.

1993
LEGO police officers got new-look uniforms as part of the LEGO Town Rescue theme, and featured individual face designs for the first time.

2019
The Sky Police fly the first LEGO City police jets, wearing all-new flight suits and oxygen masks. One officer even wears a jetpack!

Brick History

The first LEGO range to feature police elements was Town Plan, which boasted three static traffic police figures way back in 1956.

THE NAME'S DETAIN, DUKE DETAIN!

FAMOUS (AND INFAMOUS) NAMES

Since 2019, many police sets have included named characters from the LEGO City Adventures TV series, such as cops Duke DeTain and Rooky Partnur, and crooks Snake Rattler and Daisy Kaboom!

LOOK CLOSER

In 2018's Police Headquarters (set 7744), a bored crook has scrawled graffiti on the prison cell walls!

MOST WANTED

Have you seen these crooks in your minifigure collection? If so, the LEGO City Police would like to hear from you!

FUNNY HOW WE'RE ALL THE SAME HEIGHT.

First seen: **1993**   First seen: **2005**   First seen: **2015**   First seen: **2017**   First seen: **2022**

ISLAND LIFE

Welcome to Ninjago Island – where elemental powers, friendship, and finding your true potential are the keys to endless ninja adventure!

Piece particulars

Spinners send minifigures twirling into tornado-like action! They have featured in LEGO® NINJAGO® since the beginning, and the latest version has a unique, multicoloured base and a ripcord launcher on top.

REALLY?!

Temple of Airjitzu (set 70751) from 2015 was the first time that all six ninja and Master Wu appeared together in one set!

FACT STACK

The LEGO NINJAGO theme launched in 2011, with 21 sets and an animated TV series.

By the time of the theme's 10th anniversary in 2021, there were more than 300 NINJAGO sets!

In 2017, THE LEGO® NINJAGO® MOVIE™ merited its own theme, with another 20 sets (see p.214).

名誉

AWESOME! In 2020, some LEGO NINJAGO Master of the Mountains sets doubled as board games! Players moved minifigures across the squares while trying to avoid spiders, lava, and other perils.

FUN 5

LEGO NINJAGO villains' lairs

1 The Crystal King Temple (set 71771), 2022

2 Castle of the Forsaken Emperor (set 70678), 2019

3 Dragon Pit (set 70655), 2018

4 City of Stiix (set 70732), 2015

5 Garmadon's Dark Fortress (set 2505), 2011

IT'S A SIGN!

Several 2022 sets include unique printed banner pieces for the ninja to collect. Banners are earned by completing missions and acquiring new skills.

I'M ON TOP OF THIS... ROOF!

WOW!

In 2021, ultracool fashion brand HYPE launched a range of bags, tops, shorts, joggers, and jackets all based on LEGO NINJAGO!

LOOK CLOSER

Many NINJAGO sets include signs and messages written in the local language, Ninjargon. A chart in Ninja Dojo Temple (set 71767) shows how to translate Ninjargon into English!

Brick History

The LEGO NINJAGO theme was originally planned to end in 2013, with sets from that year labelled "The Final Battle". Happily, they proved so popular that new sets keep on coming to this day!

WHAT'S COOKING?

Minifigures need a broad and balanced diet if they're to grow up to be four bricks high! Happily, there's a world of dining options for them to choose from.

FACT STACK

Over the years, minifigures and mini dolls have dined at pizzerias, bakeries, cupcake cafés, and more.

The Newbury Juice Bar (set 40336) from 2019's LEGO® Hidden Side™ range could transform into a monster!

The most popular place to eat in Ninjago City is Chen's Noodle House – even though its owner is a master villain!

MOST SUPERSIZED SNACK

A giant donut sign in 2019's Donut Shop Opening (set 60233)

FUN 5

Most popular minifigure-scale fruit and veg

1 **Cherries** are on top – in more than 300 sets.

2 Red and green **apples** appear in more than 280 sets.

3 **Carrots** sprout up in more than 160 different sets.

4 **Bananas** slip into more than 150 sets.

5 **Pumpkins** aren't just for Halloween, in more than 40 sets.

Q Do minifigures like ice cream?

A No, they don't like it, they love it! The ice-cream cone element has appeared in almost 250 sets since 2013, including LEGO City's Ice-Cream Truck (set 60253). Ice-cream scoops feature in more than 175 sets – in nine different colours!

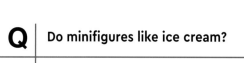

AWESOME!

Food plays a big part in the LEGO® Monkie Kid™ theme – from flower fruit and moon cake to Pigsy's battle-ready restaurant, the Noodle Tank!

IT'S A SIGN!

The LEGO® Friends love tucking in to tacos at 2022's Street Food Market (set 41701). Perhaps that's why the giant taco sign looks a little worried!

SNACK BAR

1979

The first minifigure Snack Bar (set 675) opens, serving ice cream, coffee, and much more.

REALLY?!

No wonder minifigures eat out so much. LEGO City didn't get its first Grocery Store (set 60347) until 2022!

1980

Citizens snack on fish and chips in Town Square Castle Scene (set 1592). The Dutch version of this set serves "soup und wurst".

1983

A Hamburger Stand (set 6683) arrives in LEGOLAND Town, serving burgers in the form of 1×1 tiles!

1990

LEGOLAND Town gets its first sit-down restaurant with the romantic-looking Breezeway Café (set 6376).

McCHILL Ice Cream

HOW MANY CAN I GET WITH THIS?

Piece particulars

The LEGO Friends theme was the first to use a decorated minifigure head as a pineapple.

LOOK CLOSER

Traditional treats for minifigures in 2020's Chinese New Year Temple Fair (set 80105) include candied hawthorn and steamed buns with printed faces!

OUT OF THIS WORLD

The LEGO® Space theme blasted into orbit in the 1970s. Since then it has rocketed beyond our solar system to discover ice planets, space bugs, and more!

WOW!

Robotic space bugs from the planet Zotax brought a whole new buzz to LEGO Space in the 1998 Insectoids subtheme.

FUN 5

Space bases

1 Command Centre (set 926), 1979

2 Space Supply Station (set 6930), 1983

3 Message Intercept Base (set 6987), 1988

4 Space Station Zenon (set 1793), 1995

5 Space Police Central (set 5985), 2010

SPACE BASE 1979 TO SPACE BASE 1988. OVER.

AWESOME! In 2007, the LEGO® Mars Mission subtheme used hand pumps to speed Martian figures through the base's transport tubes.

FIRST FLYING SAUCER

Spyrius Gigantic Spy UFO (set 6939)

FACT STACK

The LEGO Space race began with four sets in 1978.

The LEGO Space theme got an update in 1987, with the dawn of "Futuron".

Since 1987, there have been 21 different Space subthemes.

THERE'S NO SPACE FOR CRIME HERE.

STOP, POLICE!

In 1989, the first LEGO Space Police brought Blacktron crooks to justice, locking them up in portable prison pods.

Brick History

The 338-piece Galaxy Explorer (set 497) was the biggest LEGO Space set of the 1970s. Its lasting popularity led to a 1,254-piece update (set 10497) in 2022!

30 years of LEGO Space was celebrated in 2009 with the release of this space minifigure statue in Galactic Enforcer (set 5974).

HAPPY BIRTHDAY TO ME!

IN·ANNOS·TRIGINTA·
AD·CAELUM·INFINITUM·
CONSTRUXIT·

Q Are all LEGO Space sets based in outer space?

A No. The Alien Conquest subtheme, released in 2011, was based around an alien invasion of Earth – a first for LEGO Space.

REALLY?!

In 1990, M:Tron sets used magnets to defy gravity. Magnetic elements would later feature in Ice Planet 2002 and Spyrius sets.

FRIENDS OLD AND NEW

The LEGO® Friends theme was the first to feature mini dolls in 2012. In 2023, it welcomes a whole new generation of BFFs to its ever-growing cast of characters!

FACT STACK

The original five Friends were Andrea, Emma, Mia, Olivia, and Stephanie, who starred in sets for ten years.

The 2023 range focuses on new Friends Aliya, Autumn, Leo, Liann, Nova, Olly, Paisley, and Zac.

OLLY
Olly enjoys vlogging and bringing his friends together. He loves designing clothes and looking at the latest fashion trends!

ZAC
Zac recently moved to Heartlake City. He has a great sense of humour, and loves sports and anime. He's very energetic.

LIANN
Liann has a quirky personality. She's creative, impulsive, and never stays still for very long! She loves painting and drawing comics.

ALIYA
Aliya is a strong leader and has a busy schedule. She's studious with plenty of integrity and is a very caring person.

AWESOME!
Set in Heartlake's bustling Unity Street, 2023's Downtown Flower and Design Stores (set 41732) features the Friends theme's first furniture store and first police officer mini doll!

PAISLEY

Paisley is a talented musician, but is shy about sharing her skills. She likes to raise money for good causes, after losing her mum to illness.

WOW!

Main Street building (set 41704, below) from 2022 includes a working lift, so Harper and other wheelchair users can reach the upper floors.

FUN 5

Heartlake City pets

1 Leo's cat, Churro

2 Nova's dog, Pickle

3 Autumn's horse, Spring

4 Andrea's rabbit, Jazz

5 Olivia's hamsters, Harry, Molly, and Rumble

NOVA

Nova loves technology and gaming. She can be sharp, but is caring at heart, and volunteers with Autumn at a rescue centre for dogs.

LEO

Leo comes from a large Mexican family, and his grandmother, Gloria, has taught him to be a great cook. He also loves to play football.

Brick History

The first ever LEGO roller-coaster was the Friends Amusement Park Roller Coaster (set 41130) in 2016. It also came with a Ferris wheel and a drop tower!

AUTUMN

Autumn loves animals, the outdoors, and horse riding. She never lets having a limb difference get in the way of living her life to the fullest.

Q What happened to the original Friends when they grew up?

A Lots! Mia is Autumn's mum and now runs an organic farm, while Stephanie is the mayor of Heartlake City! Andrea and Emma followed their artistic dreams, while Olivia became a pioneering scientist.

MAKING HISTORY

Few eras in history are as fondly remembered and action-packed as the bygone age of LEGO® Castle, which included more than just LEGO castles!

FACT STACK

There have been more than 200 LEGO Castle sets since the theme launched in 1978.

The name LEGO Castle was not actually used on set packaging until 2007.

LEGO Castle Advent Calendars counted the knights until Christmas in 2008 and 2012.

JOINED-UP JOUST

The huge gatehouse in 2012's Kingdoms Joust (set 10223) is shaped so that two identical sets can be arranged back to back, creating an even more impressive building.

14

Number of LEGO Castle sets that feature fire-breathing dragons!

IT'S A SIGN! The huge shield in 2005's King's Siege Tower (set 8875) is one of the largest LEGO Castle elements. It includes a built-in LEGO brick, so you can add your own details to it.

REALLY?! More than a decade before LEGO NINJAGO, 1990s LEGO Castle sets, such as Treasure Transport (set 6033), featured the very first LEGO ninja!

CHEQUERED HISTORY

Four LEGO Castle chess sets have been released since 2005, pitching knight against dragon, king against skeleton queen, dwarf against troll, and jester against wizard!

Brick History

In 2001, two much-loved 1980s sets, Guarded Inn (set 6067) and Black Falcon's Fortress (set 6074), were reissued as "LEGO Legends" sets for a whole new generation to enjoy.

LOOK CLOSER

In 1988, LEGO Castle horses wore decorative barding for the first time. From 2005, they sometimes wore armoured headgear, too.

FUN 5

Pieces first found in LEGO Castle sets

1 Flags (1984)

2 Rocks (1992)

3 Flames (1993)

4 Bats (1997)

5 Cows (2009)

WOW!

In 1984, the LEGO Castle **Catapult** (set 6030) made use of **LEGO® Technic** parts to become the first **missile-launching** LEGO set!

HAVE YOU TRIED GETTING IN?

YES, IT MAKES THE KNIGHTS FLY BY!

CAPTURING THE CASTLES

In the Middle Ages, it took decades to build a decent castle. Since 1978, the LEGO Castle theme has shown how you can do it in just a couple of hours!

New large wall panel pieces made for quicker castle building, and allowed for printed stonework details in sets such as **King's Castle** (set 6080).

1984

1978

The first **LEGO Castle** (set 375) is unmistakable in bright yellow. Like many castles that followed, this set has hinged walls that open for easy play.

2009

The only LEGO Castle stronghold not to be controlled by knights, **Trolls' Mountain Fortress** (set 7097) has the Crown King guarded by enormous trolls.

King's Castle Siege (set 7094) blended classic LEGO Castle looks with modern play features such as catapults, a collapsing wall, and a spinning bridge.

2007

2013

The biggest enclosed LEGO fortress of the theme's original run, King's Castle (set 70404), could combine with The Gatehouse Raid (set 70402) to make it even bigger!

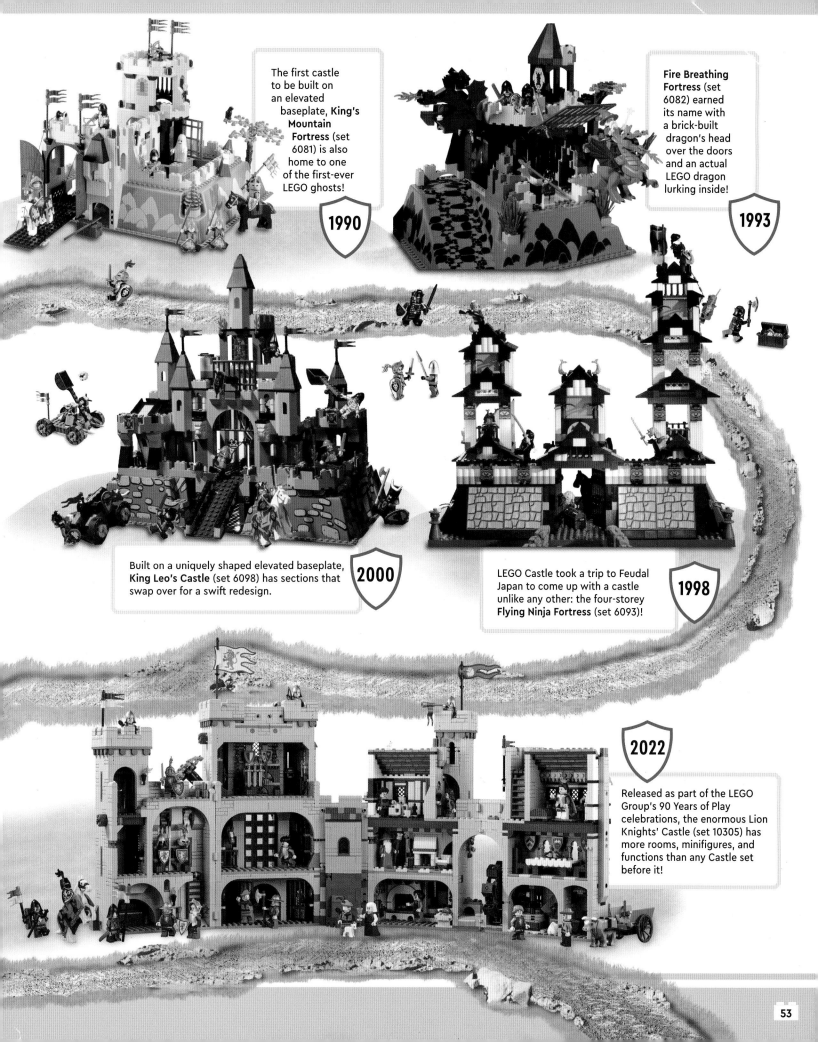

The first castle to be built on an elevated baseplate, **King's Mountain Fortress** (set 6081) is also home to one of the first-ever LEGO ghosts!

1990

Fire Breathing Fortress (set 6082) earned its name with a brick-built dragon's head over the doors and an actual LEGO dragon lurking inside!

1993

Built on a uniquely shaped elevated baseplate, **King Leo's Castle** (set 6098) has sections that swap over for a swift redesign.

2000

LEGO Castle took a trip to Feudal Japan to come up with a castle unlike any other: the four-storey **Flying Ninja Fortress** (set 6093)!

1998

2022

Released as part of the LEGO Group's 90 Years of Play celebrations, the enormous Lion Knights' Castle (set 10305) has more rooms, minifigures, and functions than any Castle set before it!

BEHIND THE MASKS

Launched under the LEGO® Technic banner in 2001, the buildable action figures of the BIONICLE® theme branched out to become a mythic multimedia phenomenon!

The BIONICLE Dictionary

Matoran: The most populous species in the BIONICLE universe. Each Matoran is linked to an element but cannot control its power.

Toa: Heroes who protect the Matoran and the Great Spirit Mata Nui by using their elemental power to fight for good.

Turaga: Former Toa who gave up their powers to become wise "elders" and lead the Matoran.

Kanohi: Masks worn by the Matoran and Toa that give them power.

Brick History

In 2005, LEGO® BIONICLE® branched out into minifigure-scale playsets. Instead of minifigures, however, the sets featured all-new figures of six Toa heroes and their Visorak foes.

THE TOA

The first six full-sized BIONICLE heroes to be introduced in 2001 belonged to the Toa tribe. New versions of all six were released in 2016.

GALI

Toa of Water (set 71307)

KOPAKA

Toa of Ice (set 71311)

POHATU

Toa of Stone (set 71306)

1 The monstrous **Makuta**

2 The deep-sea-dwelling **Barraki**

3 The greedy, grimacing **Piraka**

4 The extra-scary **Skull Army**

5 The big, bad **Elemental Beasts**

Piece particulars

Most LEGO BIONICLE characters come with a special Kanohi mask piece, many of which are exclusive to just one set.

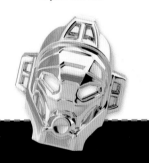

Brick statistics

BIONICLE media

50 comics
also collected as graphic novels

48 books
including stories and guides

6 video games
plus four mobile games

4 DVD movies
starting with the *Mask of Light* in 2003

1 Netflix series
LEGO BIONICLE: *The Journey to One*

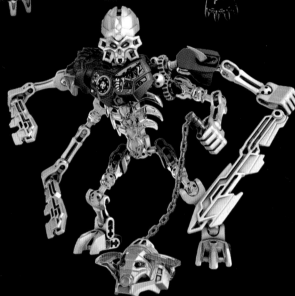

REALLY?!
The islands and cities where LEGO BIONICLE adventures take place are all located on the giant body of an ancient being called Mata Nui!

ONUA
Toa of Earth (set 71309)

LEWA
Toa of Air (71305)

TAHU
Toa of Fire (set 71308)

MONKEY TALES

With its roots in ancient Chinese folklore, the LEGO® Monkie Kid™ theme puts a modern spin on timeless tales for a worldwide audience.

LONG LIVE THE KING

The Monkey King is an important figure in Chinese folklore and appears in various forms throughout the Monkie Kid theme. These include Baby Monkey King, Apprentice Monkey King, Warden Monkey King, and Battle Monkey King (pictured).

LOOK CLOSER

The Legendary Flower Fruit Mountain (set 80024) from 2021 isn't just an epic adventure set. It also tells the story of the Monkey King's life, from the moment he hatched from a giant stone egg!

REALLY?!

The fearsome Demon Bull King figure in The Flaming Foundry (set 80016) is made from 152 pieces – including four black sausage pieces as his ribcage!

FUN 5
Members of Team Monkie Kid

1. **Monkie Kid** (MK) is a noodle delivery boy chosen to battle demons!

2. MK's best friend, **Mei**, is gifted with ancestral dragon powers!

3. **Sandy** might look scary, but he just wants a quiet and peaceful life.

4. Noodle shop owner **Pigsy** is MK's friend as well as his boss.

5. **Mo** is Sandy's pet cat, as their shared hairstyle suggests!

AWESOME!

The epic City of Lanterns (set 80036) from 2022 is packed full of cool places for Monkie Kid to hang out – including a LEGO Store stocking Monkie Kid sets!

Piece particulars

New minifigure parts introduced for the Monkie Kid theme include the hero's headphones, Princess Iron Fan's horn-like hair, and the Bull Clones' helmets.

Brick statistics

The Heavenly Realms (set 80039), 2022

3 stories in one set
The Monkey King's adventures in the Peach Garden, the Furnace, and the Palace

2,433 pieces
Making it the biggest Monkie Kid set to date

8 minifigures
Including three versions of the Monkey King himself

4 new flexible cloud pieces
Pull them to the sides to see the heavens open

1 golden bridge
Made from a roller-coaster track element

FACT STACK

Launched in 2020, LEGO Monkie Kid is inspired by the 16th-century Chinese novel *Journey to the West*.

No one knows who wrote *Journey to the West*, which is itself based on much older Chinese folk tales.

The Monkie Kid story begins when an ordinary boy is chosen to wield the Monkey King's golden staff...

ANYTHING IS POSSIBLE

Make-believe is at the heart of every LEGO® play theme – but some are more fantastical than others! In these worlds, magic, mystery, and special powers are at the heart of the story...

LEGO® LEGENDS OF CHIMA™

Set in a world where competing animal tribes gain powers from a mystical energy called CHI, LEGO Legends of Chima spanned more than 100 sets and almost 150 minifigures from 2013 to 2015. Its heroes included Laval the Lion, Eris the Eagle, and Fluminox the Phoenix.

LEGO® ELVES

The first fantasy theme to feature mini dolls, LEGO Elves followed the adventures of Emily Jones, a human girl who travels through a portal to a world of elves, dragons, and goblins. More than 30 magical sets were released in the theme between 2015 and 2018.

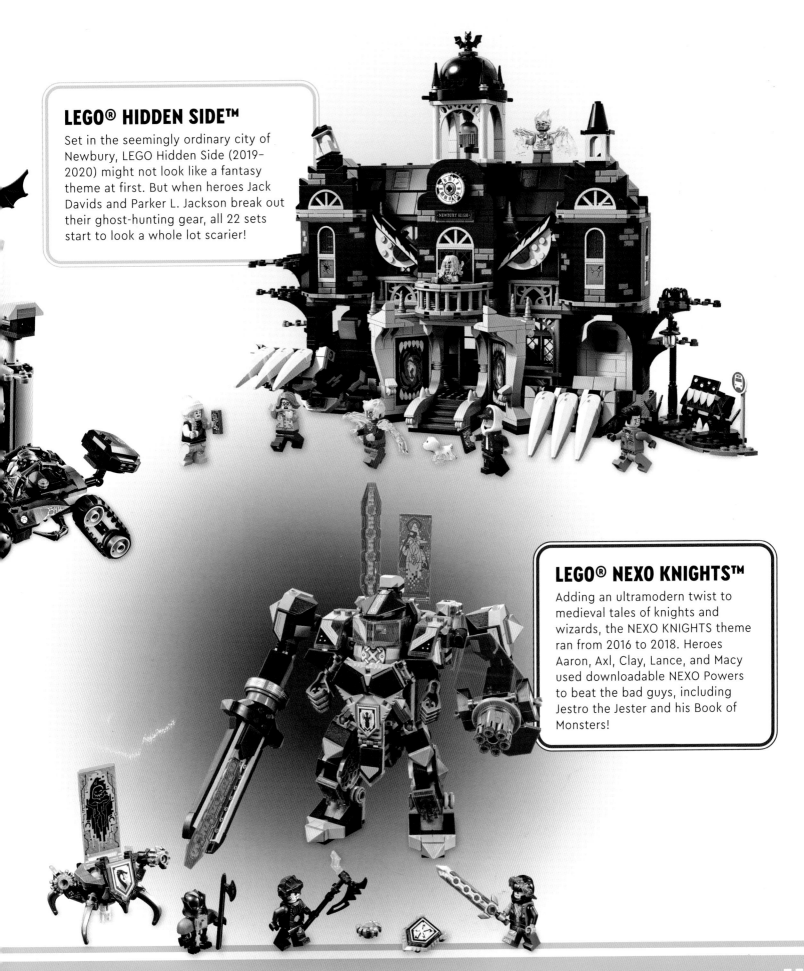

LEGO® HIDDEN SIDE™

Set in the seemingly ordinary city of Newbury, LEGO Hidden Side (2019–2020) might not look like a fantasy theme at first. But when heroes Jack Davids and Parker L. Jackson break out their ghost-hunting gear, all 22 sets start to look a whole lot scarier!

LEGO® NEXO KNIGHTS™

Adding an ultramodern twist to medieval tales of knights and wizards, the NEXO KNIGHTS theme ran from 2016 to 2018. Heroes Aaron, Axl, Clay, Lance, and Macy used downloadable NEXO Powers to beat the bad guys, including Jestro the Jester and his Book of Monsters!

AWESOME!

In 2012, LEGO minifigure paramedics stopped wearing white and suited up in bright red gear with reflective silver safety stripes.

REALLY?!

The slightly scary operating room in 2006's LEGO City Hospital (set 7892) includes a robot claw hand, a buzz saw, and a chainsaw!

Piece particulars

Minifigure gurneys with hinged wheel pieces appeared in more than 30 sets between 1985 and 2011, when they were replaced by stretchers without wheels.

IT'S A SIGN!

Stickers in 1978's Hospital (set 231) include weighing scales, surgical gear, observation charts, and a chart for eye tests.

WOW!

In 2022, LEGO City got a hospital with a maternity ward, an MRI scanner, and a resident clown!

FUN 5

Air ambulances

1 Red Cross Helicopter (set 626), 1978

2 Med-Star Rescue Plane (set 6356), 1988

3 Rescue Helicopter (set 7903), 2006

4 Ambulance Plane (set 60116), 2016

5 Ambulance Helicopter (set 60179), 2018

WE SHOULD SEE A DOCTOR ABOUT THIS!

PRICKLIEST PATIENT

Hedgehog from Mia's Vet Clinic (set 10728)

I STUDIED MEDICINE IN VEIN.

INJECTION MOULDING

The first LEGO medic to carry a hypodermic needle was the LEGO Minifigures Nurse in 2010. The small syringe is not sharp and has now appeared in more than 30 sets.

Brick History

In 1975, the first LEGO Hospital (set 363) featured the forerunners to modern minifigures, including two who were built into the stretcher they were carrying!

Piece particulars

First seen in 2018's LEGO Friends Heartlake Hospital (set 41318), a special bandage piece can be worn by mini dolls and minifigures alike.

FACT STACK

Minifigure medics debuted in Ambulance (set 606) and Red Cross Car (set 623) in 1978.

The first minifigure hospital was LEGO Town's Paramedic Unit (set 6364) in 1980.

Hospitals, ambulances, and doctors have appeared in LEGO® Fabuland and LEGO DUPLO sets.

GET WELL SOON

In the action-packed worlds of LEGO® Town, LEGO® City, and Heartlake City, it's good to know there's always a minifigure medic on call, and an ambulance is never far away!

BUILDING SIGHTS

Thanks to LEGO® Architecture and other advanced building themes, you can now enjoy the world's most impressive buildings from the comfort of your own home.

> LET ME LIGHT YOUR WAY AROUND THESE FAMOUS SIGHTS.

STATUE OF LIBERTY, USA

In 2000, a LEGO Sculptures set used 2,847 sand green pieces to depict an 84 cm (33 in)-high Statue of Liberty (set 3450).

84 CM (33 IN)

SAN FRANCISCO, USA

Though only eight studs deep, 2019's LEGO Architecture San Francisco skyline (set 21043) creates an illusion of depth with its cleverly scaled Golden Gate Bridge.

San Francisco

29 CM (11 IN)

THE GREAT PYRAMID OF GIZA, EGYPT

The outer walls lift off 2022's LEGO Architecture Great Pyramid of Giza (set 21058) to reveal some of the ancient techniques used to construct the real thing!

EMPIRE STATE BUILDING, USA

The Art Deco Skyscraper, opened in New York City in 1931. The LEGO Architecture Empire State Building (set 21046) features four highly detailed facades and six yellow cabs on Fifth Avenue.

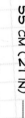

55 CM (21 IN)

35 CM (14 IN)

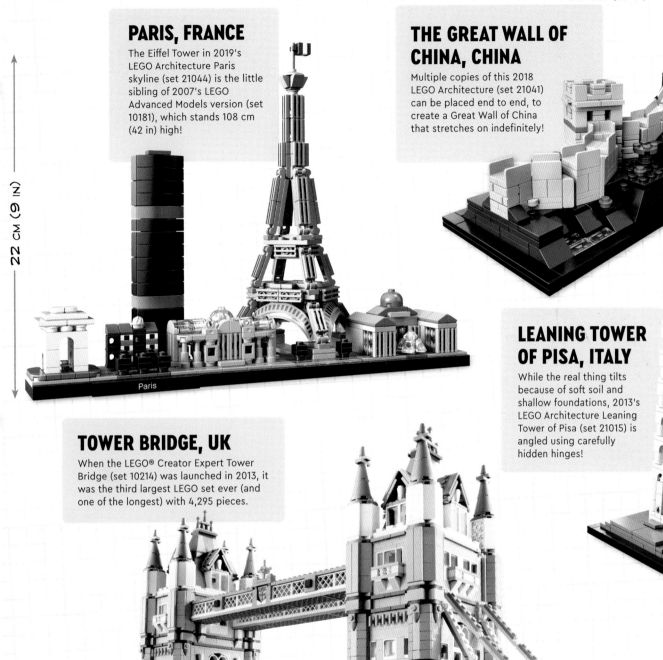

PARIS, FRANCE

The Eiffel Tower in 2019's LEGO Architecture Paris skyline (set 21044) is the little sibling of 2007's LEGO Advanced Models version (set 10181), which stands 108 cm (42 in) high!

THE GREAT WALL OF CHINA, CHINA

Multiple copies of this 2018 LEGO Architecture (set 21041) can be placed end to end, to create a Great Wall of China that stretches on indefinitely!

27 CM (11 IN)

22 CM (9 IN)

LEANING TOWER OF PISA, ITALY

While the real thing tilts because of soft soil and shallow foundations, 2013's LEGO Architecture Leaning Tower of Pisa (set 21015) is angled using carefully hidden hinges!

26 CM (10 IN)

TOWER BRIDGE, UK

When the LEGO® Creator Expert Tower Bridge (set 10214) was launched in 2013, it was the third largest LEGO set ever (and one of the longest) with 4,295 pieces.

102 CM (40 IN)

FIRE POWER

Though the first LEGO® flame piece wasn't introduced until 1993, LEGO fire service sets have been around since the 1950s and are still burning brightly today.

WOW!

Fire Helicopter Response (set 60248) from 2020 comes with a 'copter that really flies when you pull its ripcord launcher!

HOW DO I LAND THIS THING?

FUN 5
Burning builds through time

1 Abandoned sardine factory
Fire Brigade (set 60321), 2022

2 Science lab
Fire Command Unit (set 60282), 2021

3 Burger bar sign
Burger Bar Fire Rescue (set 60214), 2019

4 TV satellite tower
Fire Utility Truck (set 60111), 2016

5 Lighthouse
Fire Boat (set 60109), 2016

REALLY?!

When LEGO City Fire Chief Freya McCloud isn't at work, she likes to perform stunts on her Fire Stunt Bike (set 60311)!

FACT STACK

The first LEGO Fire Station (set 1308) was part of the Town Plan sets in 1957.

The largest LEGO fire truck is a 1,035-piece LEGO Technic vehicle (set 8289) from 2006.

The smallest fire truck is a nine-piece toy in Winter Holiday Train (set 10254) from 2016.

AWESOME!

Since 2016, many LEGO City Fire sets have featured stud-shooting hose pieces for firing "water" at the towering flames.

Q Are all LEGO fire engines red?

A No. Launch Evac 1 (set 6614) from LEGO Town's 1995 Launch Command subtheme is white, and 2006's LEGO City Airport Fire Truck (set 7891) is yellow.

IT'S A SIGN!

The LEGO City Fire Department has had four different logos since 2005. The latest has been seen in several stylish colour variations since 2019.

Piece particulars

The transparent blue pieces that are used to show a spray of water are the same shape as the transparent orange pieces used to represent flames.

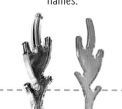

12

Number of LEGO fireboats that really float on water.

POLE TO POLE

The 2016 LEGO City Fire Station (set 60110) was the first to feature a corkscrew-style fire pole that minifigures can really slide down. The much-loved set was updated as Fire Station Headquarters (set 77944) in 2021, still with the same pole design.

WHEEEEE!

HERE BE PIRATES!

Avast ye landlubbers – be on the lookout, there be LEGO® Pirates about! Since 1989, this scurvy crew have been causing trouble across the seven seas.

FACT STACK

LEGO Pirates was the first theme to vary the original minifigure face design, introducing beards, eyepatches, and more.

Notable LEGO Pirates include Captain Redbeard, Captain Brickbeard, and the Pirate Queen (pictured).

Pirates also plundered their way into the LEGO DUPLO range in 2006!

WOW!

The first wave of Pirates sets in 1989 included a comic-book and minifigure set, telling a timber-shivering tale called *The Golden Medallion*!

LAND AHOY!

Not all LEGO Pirates adventures take place at sea! Trading posts, island hideouts, and strongholds such as Eldorado Fortress (set 6276, pictured) were all part of the piratical action from the start.

WHY ARE PIRATES CALLED PIRATES?

THEY JUST AARRR!

FUN 5

Factions pitted against the Pirates

 **1** Bluecoats (1989)

 **2** Redcoats (1992)

 **3** Islanders (1994)

 **4** Conquistadors (1996)

 **5** Rebooted Redcoats (2009)

MOST CIVILIZED SKIRMISH

Pirates Chess Set (set 40158)

Brick History

Winter 2009 was the season for swashbuckling, as the LEGO Pirates got their own Advent Calendar (set 6299), counting down December with sawfish, skeletons, monkeys, and mermaids!

Piece particulars

LEGO Pirates sets were the first to feature monkey figures, parrot pieces, sharks, and cannons that really fire!

SHIP, SHIP, HOORAY!

The first LEGO Pirates ship was Black Seas Barracuda (set 6285) in 1989. Buccaneering builders loved it so much that it was rereleased in 2002, and reimagined as a LEGO® Ideas shipwreck (Pirates of Barracuda Bay, set 21322) in 2020!

IT'S A SIGN!

The LEGO Pirates fly their fearsome flag in more than 40 sets. In 2015, they swapped the classic skull and crossbones design for a skull and crossed swords variant.

FUN 5

LEGO coast guard rescue stations

1 LEGOLAND Town Coastal Rescue Base (set 6387), 1989

2 LEGO Town Hurricane Harbour (set 6338), 1995

3 LEGO World City Coast Watch HQ (set 7047), 2003

4 LEGO City Coast Guard Platform (set 4210), 2008

5 LEGO City Coast Guard Head Quarters (set 60167), 2017

REALLY?!

LEGO City Coast Guard Patrol (set 60014) from 2013 features more grisly grey sharks than any other LEGO set.

Brick History

In 1998, the LEGO Town Res-Q team provided coast guard and other emergency response services in vehicles such as the Res-Q Cruiser (set 6473).

Piece particulars

Life got easier for the LEGO coast guard in 1990 with the invention of the first minifigure lifejacket. Ring-shaped lifebuoys followed in 1999.

AWESOME!

In 2013, the LEGO City coast guard got a new look, a new logo, and its first proper Coast Guard Plane (set 60015).

INCUBATION STATION

It's not just minifigures that need to be kept safe at the seaside! In 2022's Beach Lifeguard Station (set 60328), the locals also keep a close watch over a clutch of turtle eggs.

MOST LAID-BACK LIGHTHOUSE

LEGO Paradisa Dolphin Point (set 6414) from 1995

2

versions of Coast Guard Station were released in the 1970s (sets 369 and 575). The second was staffed by some of the very first minifigures!

LEGO
Coast Guard Station

575

LOOK CLOSER

The LEGO Minifigures line got its first Lifeguard in 2010. Going by the initials on her swimsuit, she may just share a name with former LEGO Design Master Gitte Thorsen!

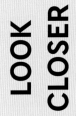

FACT STACK

Before LEGO Town got its own coast guard, it had 1985's Rescue-I Helicopter (set 6697).

C26 Sea Cutter (set 4022) from 1996 was the first coast guard ship to really float on water.

The LEGO Friends do lifeguard duty in several beach-themed sets.

TO THE RESCUE

When LEGO® Town and City minifigures stray too far from shore, the LEGO coast guard and lifeguards are ready to sail, swim, and soar into action!

DIVE IN!

LEGO® themes went into space and back in time before they ventured underwater. But when they finally took the plunge, these subaquatic sets really made a splash!

SUCKERS!

LEGO® Aquazone Hydronauts craft could pick things up using limpet-like suction cups. These special pieces have never appeared in any other theme.

FACT STACK

The first underwater-themed sets featured the LEGO Town Divers in 1987.

In the 1990s, a futuristic deep-sea theme known as "Sea-Tron" was planned but not released.

The 1997 LEGO Town Divers Shark Attack (set 6599) was originally released without any sharks!

WOW!

The 1997 LEGO Town set Deep Sea Bounty (set 6559) features a brick-built whale skeleton. Its tail is made from an aeroplane piece.

Brick History

In 2016, the world's most famous colourful watercraft was made into a LEGO Ideas set – The Beatles Yellow Submarine (set 21306)!

DEEP, MAN.

FUN 5

Deep-sea dwellers from the LEGO® Atlantis theme

1 Squid Warrior (set 8061)

2 Barracuda Guardian (set 7985)

3 Hammerhead Warrior (set 7984)

4 Lobster Guardian (set 7985)

5 Manta Warrior (set 8073)

The LEGO Aquazone Aquasharks styled their ships with scary stick-on eyes and teeth – plus a surprisingly smiley shark logo!

THIS PLACE IS A REAL DIVE.

KEY DATES

1995
The first dedicated underwater theme, LEGO Aquazone pitches the brave, crystal-hunting Aquanauts against various enemy factions until 1998.

2007
Almost sharing its name with an Aquazone faction, Aqua Raiders is a new theme in which treasure hunters tackle scary sea monsters!

2010
LEGO Atlantis explorers set out to find the fabled lost city of Atlantis, meeting many strange creatures along the way.

2015
The LEGO City Deep Sea Explorers subtheme gives subaquatic sets a more lifelike makeover, with realistic 21st-century subs.

2021
LEGO NINJAGO gets in on the underwater action with the Seabound series of sets, including the enormous Hydro Bounty.

5

Number of disc-shaped treasure keys needed to unlock the mythical Portal of Atlantis (set 8078) from the LEGO Atlantis theme.

Piece particulars

Crystal pieces were created especially for the LEGO Aquazone theme in 1995, and have since appeared in almost 250 sets.

REALLY?!

A digested diver can be seen inside the squid in 2007's LEGO® Aqua Raiders Aquabase Invasion (set 7775). His skeleton still has its diving mask on!

HOME SWEET HOME

Who wouldn't want to live in a LEGO® house? There's an endless range to choose from, and you never need to move when you can just rebuild!

FACT STACK

The LEGO Town Plan sets of the 1950s featured small homes built with about 20 bricks each.

In the 1960s and 1970s, sets such as House with Car (set 346) depicted realistic homes.

Since 2007, LEGO Creator sets have included townhouses, beach houses, treehouses, and even a skateboarder's house!

MOVING HOME

In 1973, the same stylish house was released as Swiss Villa (set 540) in the USA, Villa Mallorca in Denmark, and Italian Villa (set 356) in the rest of Europe!

REALLY?!

In some LEGO catalogues, Lionel Lion's Lodge (set 3678) from the 1982 **Fabuland** range was known as "The Story of the **Noisy Neighbours**"!

HAS ANYONE GOT ABOUT 50 EARPLUGS?

FUN 5
LEGO Town vacation villas

1 Summer Cottage (set 6365), 1981

2 Holiday Home (set 6374), 1983

3 Weekend Home (set 6370), 1985

4 Vacation House (set 1472), 1987

5 Poolside Paradise (set 6416), 1992

WRITING HOME

In 2015, a LEGO house that was really a Pencil Pot (set 40154) came with a builder working on the roof – maybe to stop any more pencils getting in!

SWEETEST RETREAT

Gingerbread House (set 40139)

Brick statistics

LEGO® Monster Fighters Haunted House (set 10228)

2,064 petrifying pieces
Including bat, snake, and spider elements

3 spine-chilling storeys
Standing a scary 39 cm (15 in) tall

17 woeful windows
12 of which are badly boarded up

4 macabre minifigure zombie heads
Built into the frightful front porch

2 glow-in-the-dark ghosts
But the vampire owners don't seem to mind

I'M THE HEAD OF THIS HOUSEHOLD!

The LEGO Friends theme is full of unique homes that reflect Heartlake City's diverse population, including Autumn's farmhouse-style home (set 41730).

AWESOME!

JOINED-UP THINKING

Since 2007, LEGO® Modular Buildings have brought new levels of detail to the minifigure-scale world. Each one is designed to slot seamlessly onto the next, in any combination you care to choose!

WOW!
A LEGO fan clearly lives in 2017's Assembly Square (set 10255). One room contains micro-scale models of LEGO sets such as the Eiffel Tower.

REALLY?!
Built into the details of Detective's Office (set 10246) from 2015 are all the clues you need to solve a cookie-smuggling mystery.

Piece particulars
There is at least one white street lamp in every Modular Building to date. LEGO Set Designer Jamie Berard promised to keep using the piece to save it from being retired!

IT'S A SIGN!

Customers of 2019's Corner Garage (set 10264) can fill their petrol tanks from an old-fashioned pump, printed with a retro version of LEGO Town's Octan Gas logo.

KEY DATES

2007
Café Corner (set 10182) becomes the first set in the LEGO Modular Building theme.

2009
Fire Brigade (set 10197) is the first Modular Building to come with a vehicle.

2012
Town Hall (set 10224) launches as the tallest Modular Building – a record it still holds.

2014
Parisian Restaurant (set 10243) proves so popular it remains available for six whole years!

LOOK CLOSER

An "out of order" launderette washing machine is actually a back way into the bank vault for a spot of literal money laundering in 2016's Brick Bank (set 10251).

Q Is Market Street a Modular Building?

A Though 2007's Market Street (set 10190) was released as part of the LEGO® Factory theme, it was designed to fit the Modular format. It is now recognized as the second entry in the Modular Buildings series.

The "sunburst" sign over the door of Café Corner (set 10182) is made by fanning out minifigure skis on a curving tube.

1891

The build date commemorated on the Town Hall (set number 10224) is also the year that LEGO Group founder Ole Kirk Kristiansen was born.

FACT STACK

The floors of each Modular Building lift away easily for access to dozens more details inside.

All minifigures in the first 12 Modular Buildings have the original 1970s smiling face design.

"Modular Building Collection" branding was introduced in 2021. Earlier sets were part of the Creator Expert line.

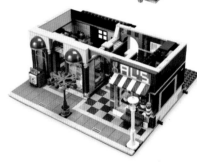

AWESOME!

2011
The 4,002-piece Assembly Square (set 10255) celebrates 10 years of Modular Buildings.

2018
Downtown Diner (set 10260) adds minifigures with varied facial expressions to the theme.

2022
Boutique Hotel (set 10297) marks the Modular Building theme's 15th anniversary with numerous nods to the past.

LEGO® *STAR WARS*™ WORLDS

WATCH OUT FOR THAT WRITING!

The LEGO® Star Wars™ theme launched in 1999 alongside the release of Star Wars: Episode I The Phantom Menace. From the beginning, the theme featured sets based around the classic trilogy of Star Wars films as well as the prequels. To date, there have been more than 650 LEGO Star Wars sets, based on 11 movies, 10 TV shows, three video games, and a theme park! LEGO Star Wars is now the longest-running licensed LEGO theme and will celebrate its quarter-century in 2024...

REALLY?!

It's not all action in the LEGO *Star Wars* universe! One 2022 set shows Luke's Aunt Beru cooking in the Lars Family Homestead Kitchen (set 40531).

BADDEST BASE

Darth Vader's Castle (set 75251), 2019

Piece particulars

In 2012 and 2013, special dome pieces were used to depict 12 *Star Wars* worlds. Each one opened to reveal a playset inside!

Brick History

The first LEGO lightsaber battle took place between Jedi Master Qui-Gon Jinn and Sith Lord Darth Maul in 1999.

Brick statistics

55+ sets inspired by sandy Tatooine
Including Mos Eisley's infamous cantina

35+ sets inspired by icy Hoth
From Echo Base to motorized AT-ATs!

25+ sets inspired by lush Naboo
Packed with Gungans and battle droids!

15+ sets inspired by the forest moon of Endor
Including 2019's microscale Battle of Endor (set 40362, pictured)

SIZE MATTERS NOT

Several LEGO *Star Wars* sets have depicted characters at larger than minifigure size. These include a 46 cm (18 in) model of villainous General Grievous (set 10186) from 2008, and a 1,073-piece sculpture of The Child (set 75318) from 2020.

The trash compactor on the LEGO Death Star (set 75159) has walls that really close in on any minifigures inside!

AWESOME!

THE MAGIC OF LEGO®
HARRY POTTER™

The original LEGO® Harry Potter™ theme launched in 2001 and retired for a brief spell in 2011. Then, in 2018, the range magically reappeared, bigger and better than ever!

FUN 5

Brick-built beasts

1 **Hungarian Horntail Dragons** are fierce fire-breathers.

2 **Aragog** is an Acromantula – a giant talking spider.

3 **Erumpents** have horns filled with exploding fluid!

4 **Thunderbirds** make storms by beating their wings.

5 **Fluffy** is Hagrid's three-headed pet dog. Down boy!

Piece particulars

The golden egg in 2005's Harry and the Hungarian Horntail (set 4767) is magnetic, so Harry can swoop past and grab it with his own magnetic element.

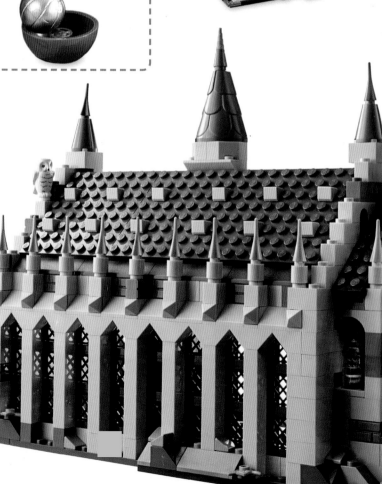

HAT'S AMAZING!

In 2001, the very first LEGO Harry Potter set, Sorting Hat (set 4701), really worked! It was built with a decorated spinning disc for sorting minifigures into the four individual Hogwarts houses.

IT'S A SIGN!

You can buy two cats for the price of one bat at Ollivanders Wand Shop in the 2011 version of Diagon Alley (set 10217)!

5972

Number of the Hogwarts Express, featured in six minifigure-scale sets since 2001.

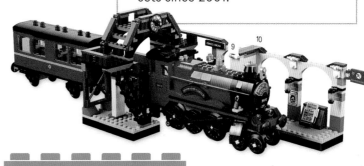

Brick History

LEGO Harry Potter launched two styles of Hogwarts Castle. During 2018–2020, sets such as Hogwarts Great Hall (set 75954) and Hogwarts Whomping Willow (set 75953) could connect together. The newer sets from 2021–2023 use a different modular system.

FACT STACK

There have been more than 100 LEGO Harry Potter sets since 2001.

There are more sets based on *Harry Potter and the Philosopher's Stone* than on any other book or film in the series.

The LEGO Harry Potter theme also includes sets based on the two *Fantastic Beasts* films.

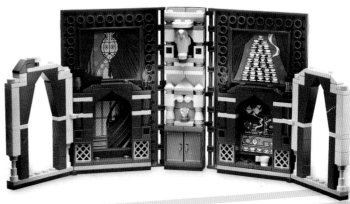

AWESOME!

Since 2021, Hogwarts Moments sets have depicted school scenes as builds that fold away to look like spell books!

JURASSIC LARKS

LEGO® dinosaur sets date back to the 1990s, but that seemed like practically prehistoric with the launch of the LEGO® Jurassic World theme in 2015!

IT'S A SIGN!

Two different printed pieces depicting a prehistoric mosquito preserved in amber have appeared in seven sets since 2015.

FACT STACK

To date, there have been almost 100 LEGO Jurassic World minifigures and more than 50 dinosaur figures.

Owen Grady and Claire Dearing feature in the most sets, with 25 and 14 appearances apiece.

Raptors are the most abundant dinosaur figures, featuring in 13 sets.

15

chest hairs on the Ian Malcolm minifigure in Jurassic Park: T. rex Rampage (set 75936)!

2001
The LEGO® Studios theme features two sets based around the filming of *Jurassic Park III*.

2015
The LEGO Jurassic World theme launches, with six sets each including at least one dinosaur.

2018
Jurassic World: Fallen Kingdom sets are joined by one based on 1993's *Jurassic Park*.

2019
The animated TV show *Jurassic World: Legend of Isla Nublar* inspires more new sets.

2022
Sets recreating the action from *Jurassic World: Dominion* feature the most new dinos since 2015!

AWESOME!
Every Jurassic World set features at least one dinosaur, but only T. rex Dinosaur Fossil Exhibition (set 76940) comes with a complete dino skeleton!

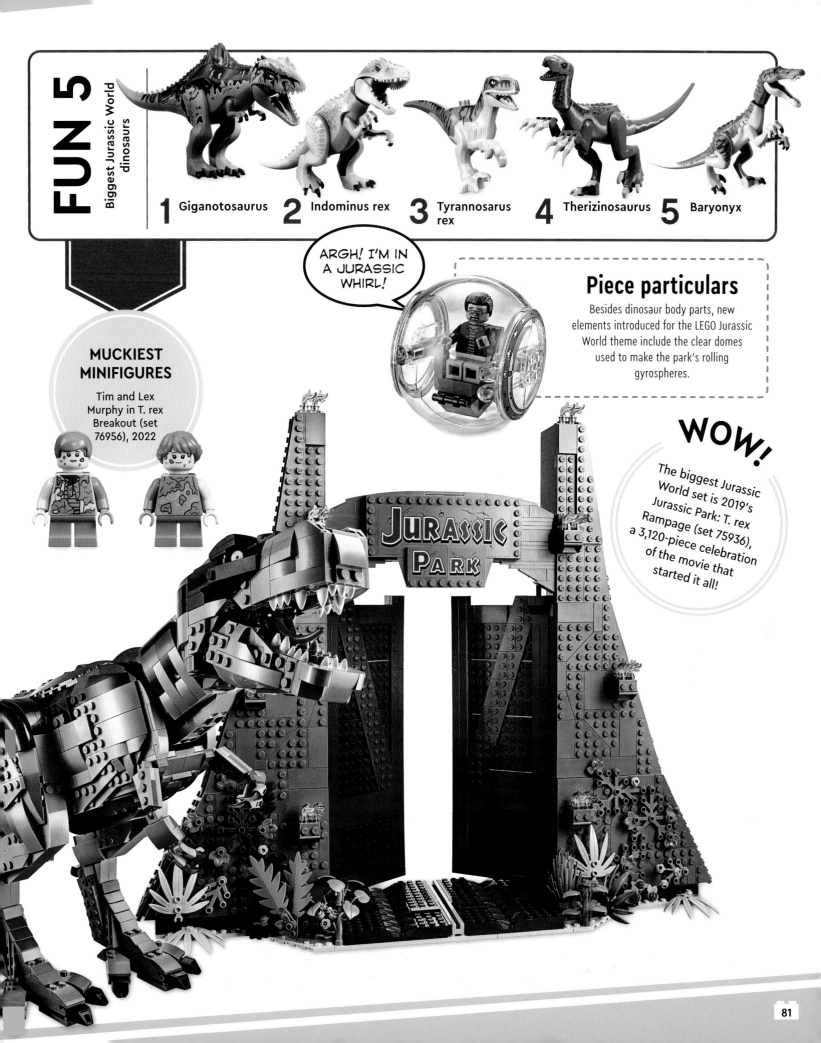

FUN 5

Biggest Jurassic World dinosaurs

1 Giganotosaurus

2 Indominus rex

3 Tyrannosaurus rex

4 Therizinosaurus

5 Baryonyx

ARGH! I'M IN A JURASSIC WHIRL!

MUCKIEST MINIFIGURES

Tim and Lex Murphy in T. rex Breakout (set 76956), 2022

Piece particulars

Besides dinosaur body parts, new elements introduced for the LEGO Jurassic World theme include the clear domes used to make the park's rolling gyrospheres.

WOW!

The biggest Jurassic World set is 2019's Jurassic Park: T. rex Rampage (set 75936), a 3,120-piece celebration of the movie that started it all!

JURASSIC PARK

AS SEEN ON SCREEN

As well as creating its own exciting worlds, the LEGO Group often teams up with film and TV studios to make sets based on big- and small-screen stories.

In 2020, the LEGO® Minifigures *Looney Tunes* series featured **Bugs Bunny** (set 71030-2), **Daffy Duck** (set 71030-7), **Petunia Pig** (set 71030-11), and that's not all, folks!

There were 18 LEGO® *Indiana Jones* sets to explore in 2008 and 2009, spanning four blockbuster movies. The first was **Indiana Jones Motorcycle Chase** (Set 7620).

The LEGO Ideas theme offered a new way to get to *Sesame Street* in 2020, with **123 Sesame Street** (set 21324). Big Bird and Elmo were among the characters included.

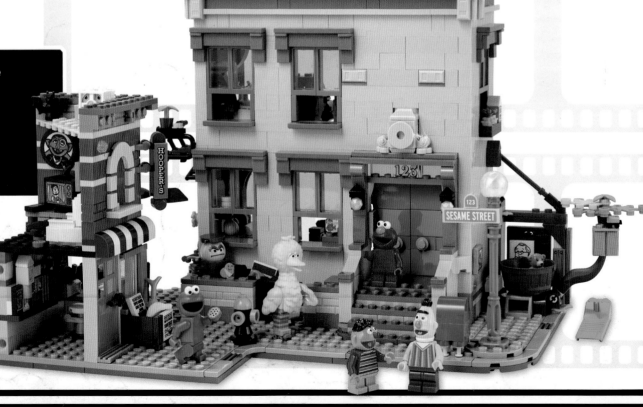

More than 25 LEGO® *The Lord of the Rings™* and LEGO® *The Hobbit™* sets were released between 2012 and 2014. The largest was the 73 cm (29 in) **Tower of Orthanc** (set 10237).

Stranger Things, Netflix's hit series, turned LEGO Upside Down in this perfectly detailed 2019 set (75810) designed for display either side up!

Sets inspired by the movie *Minions: The Rise of Gru* include 2020's Brick-built **Minions and their Lair** (set 75551). Where's the lair? Inside the opening Minion models!

Classic sitcom *Friends* has featured in two TV studio-style sets. The first was 2019's **Central Perk** (set 21319), depicting the New York pals in their favourite coffee shop.

WORLD CRAFTING

Combining virtual construction game Minecraft with real-world LEGO bricks was always going to build into something special. In 2013, the exciting LEGO® Minecraft® theme was spawned!

237

standard 2×2 bricks in the largest LEGO Minecraft set – the 2,863-piece Mountain Cave (set 21137) from 2018.

WOW!

Minecraft hero Steve has appeared as a minifigure in more than 40 sets, and became a 13 cm (5 in) "BigFig" in 2019!

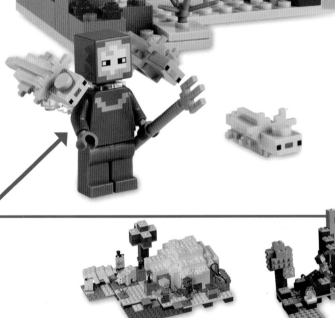

FUN 5
LEGO Minecraft biomes

1 Forest in The First Night (set 21115), 2014

2 Ocean in The Guardian Battle (set 21180), 2022

3 Snowy tundra in The Polar Igloo (set 21142), 2018

4 Nether in The Warped Forest (set 21168), 2022

AWESOME!
The first four LEGO Minecraft sets came in cube-shaped boxes that looked like Minecraft building blocks.

BIGGEST BOSS

The Ender Dragon (set 21117), 2014

WE ARE THE MOBS

"Mob" is the Minecraft name for any creature that is mobile. LEGO Minecraft features all six of the main Mob categories found in the game itself.

Sheep and Pigs are friendly **Passive Mobs**.

Piece particulars

Minifigures in the LEGO Minecraft universe have unique cube-shaped heads that are 1.5 studs wide. These pieces have no studs on top, so their helmets clutch at the sides instead.

Cave Spiders are **Neutral Mobs** that attack if provoked.

Watch out for **Hostile Mobs**, such as Zombies and Skeletons.

REALLY?!

Minecraft sets use so many 2×2 jumper plates that the LEGO Group had to make a new mould to keep up with demand.

You can befriend **Tameable Mobs**, such as Horses and Wolves.

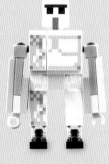

Utility Mobs, such as Iron Golems, can fight off **Hostile Mobs**.

5 Desert in The Village (set 21128), 2016

WHO'S THAT KAI?

If you think the ninja in 2020's The Illager Raid (set 21160) looks familiar, you're right. It's Kai from the LEGO NINJAGO theme, rocking a brilliant blocky Minecraft makeover!

Beware **Boss Mobs**, such as Withers, which are huge and very hostile!

IT'S-A ME, LEGO® MARIO™!

Jump into the LEGO® Super Mario™ theme and a new way to play. With interactive figures and brick-built courses, LEGO Super Mario brings the Super Mario world to life whether you're recreating your favourite scenes or building a new adventure!

FACT STACK

LEGO Super Mario play begins with a Starter Course, including an interactive LEGO® Mario™, LEGO® Luigi™, or LEGO® Peach™ figure.

Expansion Sets, Power-up Packs, and Character Packs combine with Starter Courses for more play possibilities.

Since 2020, there have been more than 30 Expansion Sets and more than 60 Character Packs!

60

seconds to get from the Start Pipe to the Goal Pole in every LEGO Super Mario timed challenge – or longer if you win a time bonus or play with two connected characters.

WOW!

Changing Mario's suit gives him different power-ups. Put him in a penguin suit, for example, and he can rack up coins just by sliding on his belly!

Piece particulars

LEGO Super Mario interactive figures are some of the most advanced LEGO elements ever made! Each one has a sensor, a speaker, and three built-in screens, so that they can have different facial expressions, play sounds, and display play info, in real time, in response to their environment.

FUN 5

Brick-built LEGO Super Mario characters

1 Lovable **Yoshi** is a lifelong friend of Mario and Luigi.

2 Level boss **Bowser Jr** just wants to be as bad as his dad!

3 No haunted mansion is complete without **King Boo**.

4 Few foes are cuter than a **Koopa Troopa**!

5 What can you say about **Toad**? He's just a fun guy...

IT'S A SIGN!

Released in 2020, the LEGO Nintendo Entertainment System (set 71374) is a 2,646-piece recreation of the classic 1980s console, plus a retro TV with moving brick-built Super Mario graphics!

REALLY?!

The biggest set in the LEGO Super Mario theme is The Mighty Bowser (set 71411), a 2,807-piece display model that can really spit a LEGO "fireball"!

AWESOME!

Special LEGO bricks known as Action Bricks are found in the LEGO Super Mario Universe. Each Action Brick makes your interactive figure respond in a different way!

A SET FOR

JANUARY

In the Chinese zodiac, 2022 was the Year of the Tiger. This commemorative big cat (set 40491) is the ninth "Year of" set released to mark the Chinese New Year.

FEBRUARY

No valentine could resist this brick-built Rose (set 852786). It's as fresh today as it was on its release in 2010.

In 2015, Valentine's Day Dinner (set 40120) came with a gold-coloured ring (or maybe a bracelet) for one lucky minifigure to wear.

MARCH – APRIL

A cuddly bunny with a bag of LEGO DUPLO bricks (set 852217) marked Easter in 2008. In 2016, a brick-built Easter Chick (set 40202) proved just as cute, if not so cuddly!

AUGUST

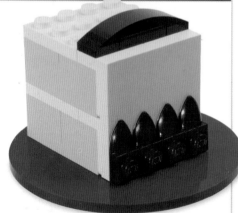

The LEGO Group's birthday is in August, and this slice of Birthday Cake (set 40048) helped it to celebrate in 2012.

SEPTEMBER

Fall Scene (set 40057) from 2013 features tree trunks you can decorate with autumnal colours – or surround with fallen leaves for minifigures to sweep up!

OCTOBER

In 2021, Halloween fans could hang this Spider and Haunted House Pack (set 40493) as part of their spine-chilling celebrations!

ALL SEASONS

MAY

May the Fourth is known as *Star Wars* Day (May the Fourth be with you – geddit?), marked by special LEGO *Star Wars* sets such as 2020's Death Star II Battle (set 40407).

JUNE

Spring turns to summer in June, and in 2013, the LEGO Group marked both seasons with the idyllic Springtime Scene (set 40052) and Summer Scene (set 40054).

JULY

US Flag (set 10042) from 2003 is one of two small stars-and-stripes builds released to mark US Independence Day, which is celebrated on 4th July.

NOVEMBER

Several LEGO sets have marked Thanksgiving in the USA, including a turkey (set 40011), a pilgrim (set 40204), and... 2014's turkey dressed as a pilgrim (set 40091)!

DECEMBER

The first Christmas set was Santa and Sleigh (set 246) in 1977. Other brick-built Santas followed, including this Santa on Skis (set 1128) from 1999.

Since 2009, winter-themed Creator sets have combined to make a snow-capped village featuring a toy shop, bakery, market, train, and even Santa's Workshop (set 10245, pictured).

A TRIP TO MINILAND

From California to Korea, the heart of each and every LEGOLAND® park is its MINILAND, a remarkable LEGO brick recreation of landmarks from around the world.

Q Do the models in MINILAND move?

A Yes. Every year, the MINILAND cars, boats, and trains at LEGOLAND Billund travel a distance equivalent to almost three trips around the world!

AWESOME! Built at 1:50 scale, the Allianz Arena soccer stadium in LEGOLAND Deutschland features more than one million bricks and 30,000 minifigure spectators.

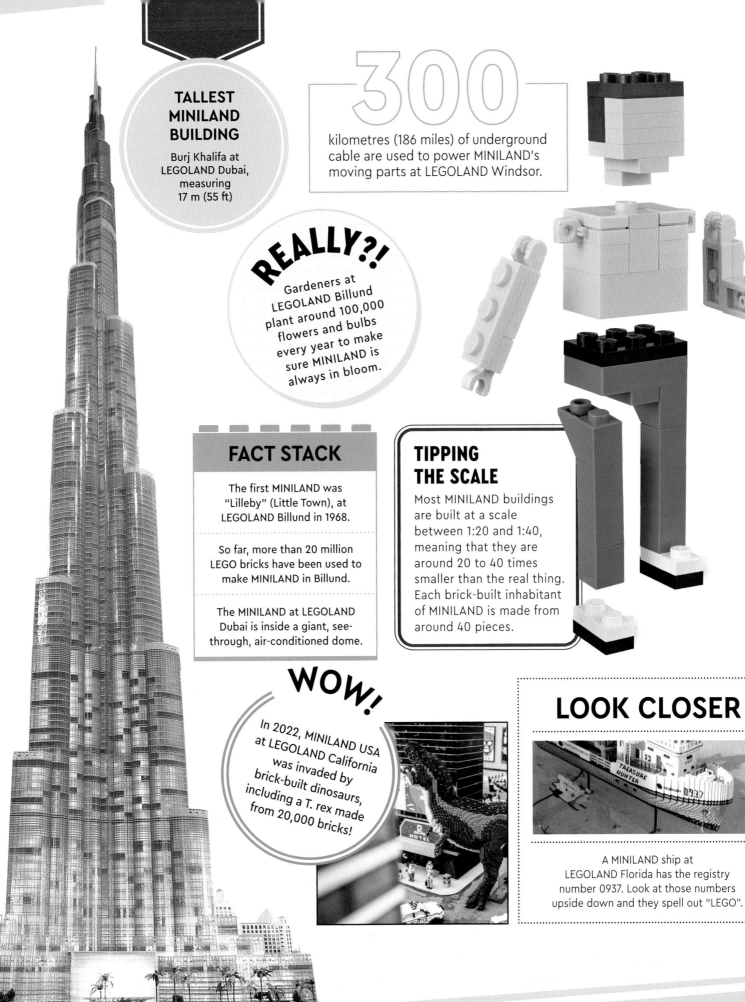

TALLEST MINILAND BUILDING

Burj Khalifa at LEGOLAND Dubai, measuring 17 m (55 ft)

300

kilometres (186 miles) of underground cable are used to power MINILAND's moving parts at LEGOLAND Windsor.

REALLY?!

Gardeners at LEGOLAND Billund plant around 100,000 flowers and bulbs every year to make sure MINILAND is always in bloom.

FACT STACK

The first MINILAND was "Lilleby" (Little Town), at LEGOLAND Billund in 1968.

So far, more than 20 million LEGO bricks have been used to make MINILAND in Billund.

The MINILAND at LEGOLAND Dubai is inside a giant, see-through, air-conditioned dome.

TIPPING THE SCALE

Most MINILAND buildings are built at a scale between 1:20 and 1:40, meaning that they are around 20 to 40 times smaller than the real thing. Each brick-built inhabitant of MINILAND is made from around 40 pieces.

WOW!

In 2022, MINILAND USA at LEGOLAND California was invaded by brick-built dinosaurs, including a T. rex made from 20,000 bricks!

LOOK CLOSER

A MINILAND ship at LEGOLAND Florida has the registry number 0937. Look at those numbers upside down and they spell out "LEGO".

CHAPTER THREE

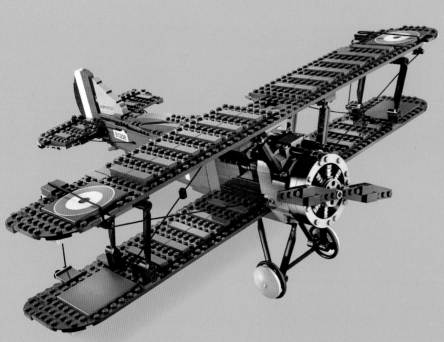

ROAD, RAIL, SEA, AND SKY

STREET LIFE

There are more than 700 vehicles in LEGO® Town and LEGO® City, and every one can take you on a million storytelling journeys!

The Town Horse Trailer (set 6359) offers two modes of transport in one set.

1986

HEY YOU, STOP HORSING AROUND!

1988

Blizzard Blazer (set 6524)

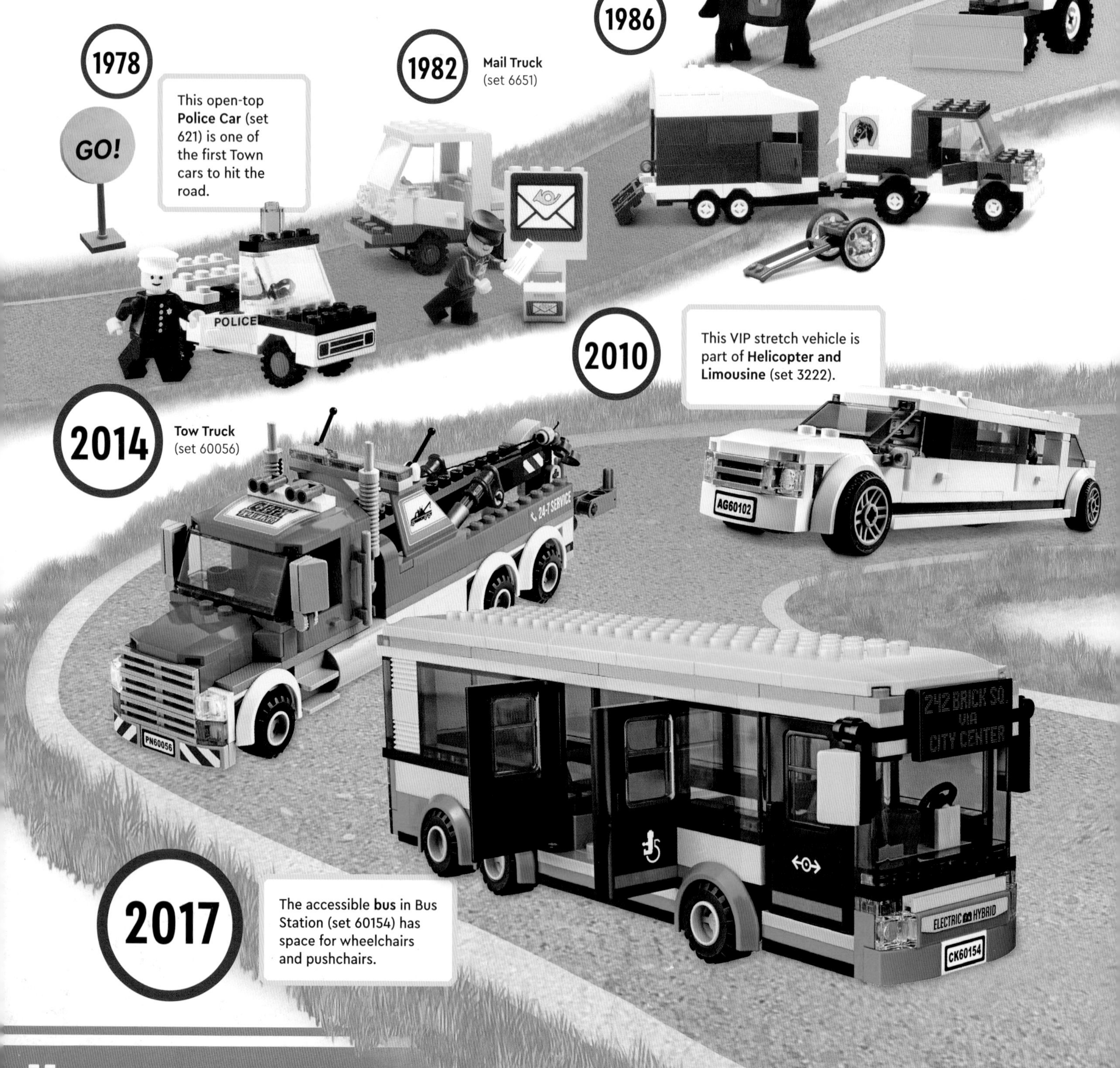

1978

This open-top **Police Car (set 621)** is one of the first Town cars to hit the road.

GO!

1982

Mail Truck (set 6651)

2010

This VIP stretch vehicle is part of **Helicopter and Limousine (set 3222)**.

AG60102

2014

Tow Truck (set 60056)

PN60056

2017

The accessible **bus** in Bus Station (set 60154) has space for wheelchairs and pushchairs.

242 BRICK SQ. VIA CITY CENTER

ELECTRIC HYBRID

CK60154

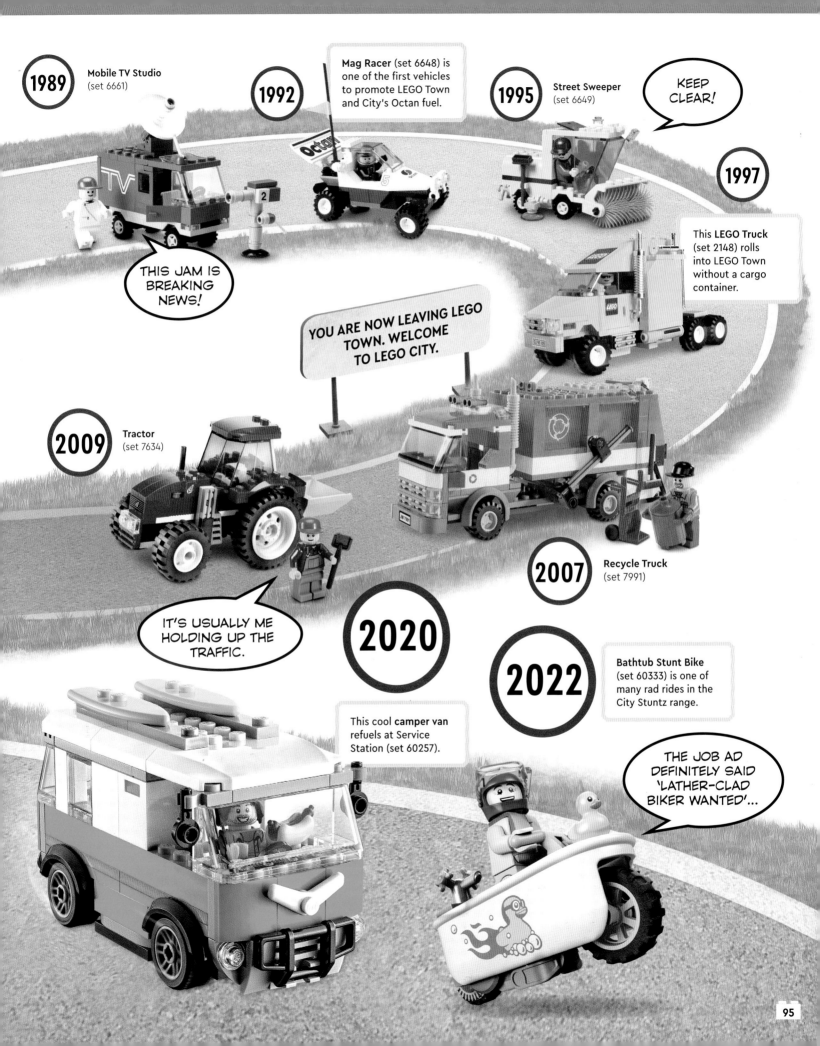

1989 Mobile TV Studio (set 6661)

1992 Mag Racer (set 6648) is one of the first vehicles to promote LEGO Town and City's Octan fuel.

1995 Street Sweeper (set 6649)

KEEP CLEAR!

1997 This LEGO Truck (set 2148) rolls into LEGO Town without a cargo container.

THIS JAM IS BREAKING NEWS!

YOU ARE NOW LEAVING LEGO TOWN. WELCOME TO LEGO CITY.

2009 Tractor (set 7634)

2007 Recycle Truck (set 7991)

IT'S USUALLY ME HOLDING UP THE TRAFFIC.

2020

This cool camper van refuels at Service Station (set 60257).

2022 Bathtub Stunt Bike (set 60333) is one of many rad rides in the City Stuntz range.

THE JOB AD DEFINITELY SAID 'LATHER-CLAD BIKER WANTED'...

LEGO Town Amazon
Crossing (set 6490), 1997

LEGO City Jungle
Mobile Lab
(set 60160), 2017

LEGO Town Arctic
Ice Surfer
(set 6579), 2000

LEGO® Friends First
Aid Jungle Bike
(set 41032), 2014

LEGO® Technic Arctic
Rescue Unit
(set 8660), 1986

SNOW AND ICE

LEGO vehicles have
been exploring the
Arctic since 1986,
using sails, skis, and
all-terrain wheels to
get around.

FORESTS
AND JUNGLE

From the LEGO Town
Outback to
Heartlake City
Jungle, minifigures
and mini dolls rely
on some heavy-duty
hardware for their
rescue missions and
scientific studies.

LEGO City Arctic
Outpost
(set 60035), 2014

Not all LEGO® vehicles are meant to stick to streets! For every cool city car, there's a mighty off-roader ready to tackle some tougher terrain.

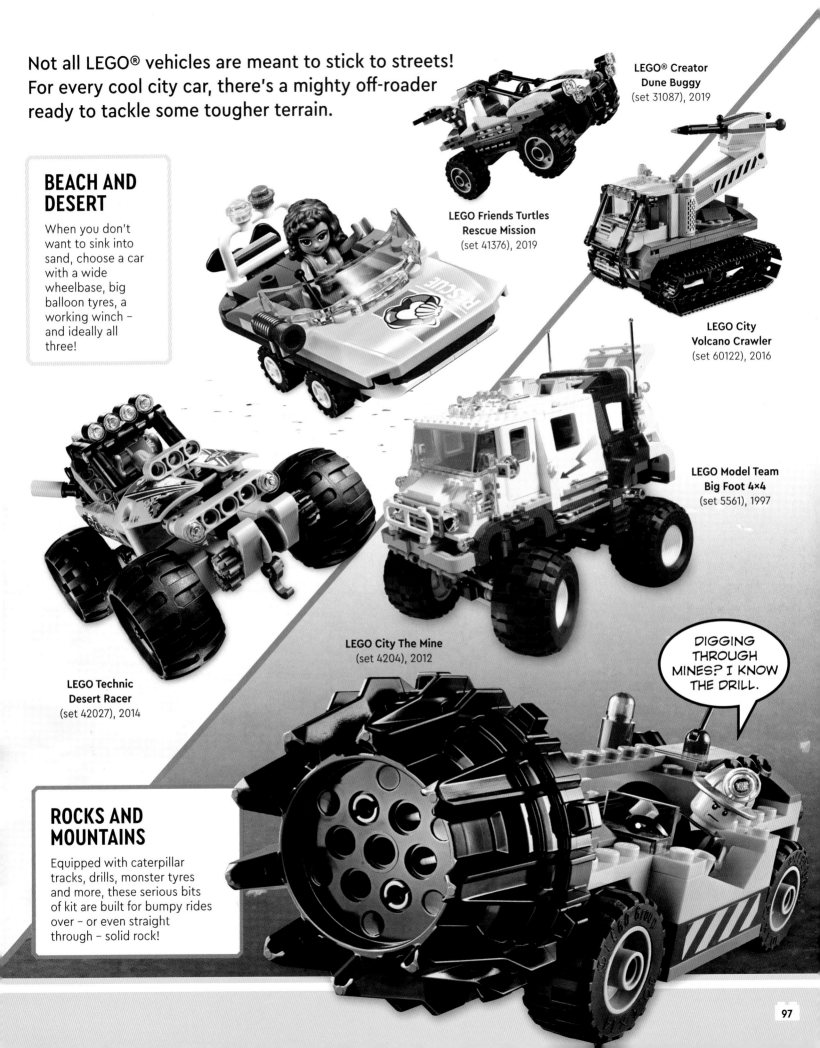

LEGO® Creator Dune Buggy (set 31087), 2019

BEACH AND DESERT

When you don't want to sink into sand, choose a car with a wide wheelbase, big balloon tyres, a working winch – and ideally all three!

LEGO Friends Turtles Rescue Mission (set 41376), 2019

LEGO City Volcano Crawler (set 60122), 2016

LEGO Model Team Big Foot 4×4 (set 5561), 1997

LEGO City The Mine (set 4204), 2012

LEGO Technic Desert Racer (set 42027), 2014

DIGGING THROUGH MINES? I KNOW THE DRILL.

ROCKS AND MOUNTAINS

Equipped with caterpillar tracks, drills, monster tyres and more, these serious bits of kit are built for bumpy rides over – or even straight through – solid rock!

CAN YOU DIG IT?

LEGO® fans love to build and rebuild, so it's no surprise that there are dozens of sets based on real-life construction and demolition vehicles!

REALLY?!

The **tipper bucket** on 2005's LEGO City Dump Truck (set 7344) **is a single piece** measuring 16 studs wide and **32 studs** long.

Piece particulars

The LEGO City Dozer (set 7685) from 2009 is one of only two sets to feature jet engine turbines but no jet engine housings.

I GET PAID FOR DOZING ON THE JOB!

WOW!

The huge LEGO City **Heavy Loader** (set 7900) from 2006 carries an **entire bridge** that can be built into your LEGO City **street system.**

FACT STACK

In 1964, the 64-piece Building Crane (set 804) was the first construction-themed vehicle.

Minifigure construction crews got to work in 1978, driving two diggers into LEGO Town.

There have been more than 50 construction-themed LEGO Technic vehicles since 1979.

Brick History

In 2012 and 2018, the LEGO City Mining subtheme featured several diggers and tippers. A special mining logo distinguishes these from similar construction vehicles.

IT'S A MINER DIFFERENCE!

55

centimetres (22 in) is the full extent of the aptly named LEGO City XXL Mobile Crane (set 7249) from 2005.

AWESOME!

The crane in 2010's LEGO City Level Crossing (set 7936) has two sets of wheels – one for roads and one for train tracks.

The familiar symbol of a worker with a shovel has featured in many LEGO sets, and even got a "Minifigures at Work" makeover in 2009's LEGO City Dump Truck (set 7631)!

Brick statistics

35 diggers and loaders
in the LEGO Town and City themes

30 dumpers, tippers, and dozers
across all of LEGO Town and City

10 mobile cranes and wreckers
in Town and City construction sets

4 cement mixers
1 in LEGO Town, 3 in LEGO City

1 Construct-o-Mech
only in the world of THE LEGO® MOVIE™!

Q | Are all LEGO construction vehicles yellow?

A | Not all! There was a blue LEGO Town Tractor (set 6504) in 1988 and an orange digger in LEGO City Juniors Road Work Truck (set 10683) in 2015.

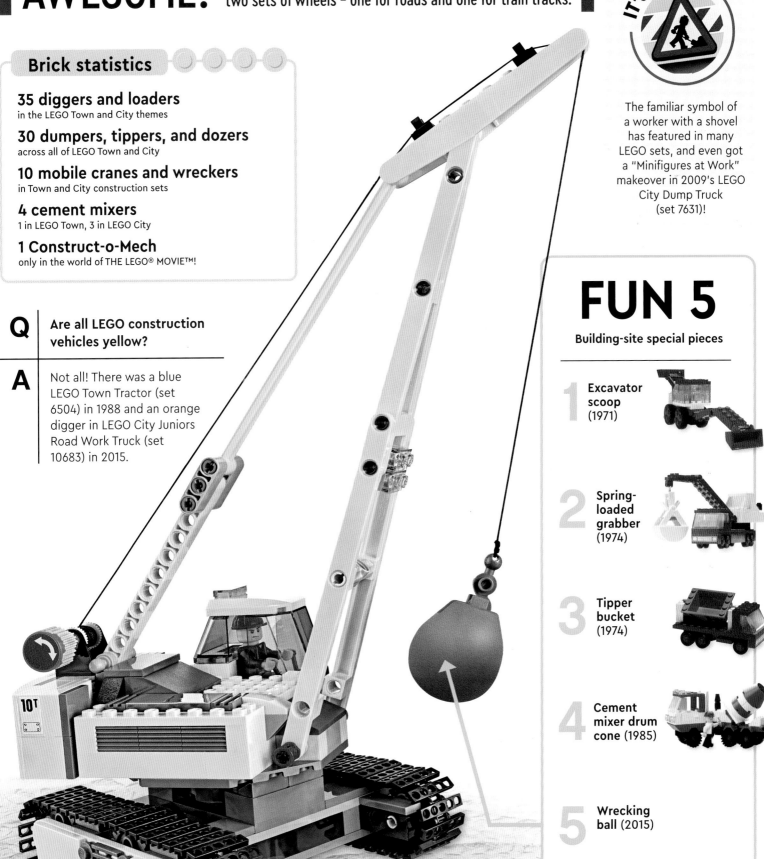

FUN 5

Building-site special pieces

1 Excavator scoop (1971)

2 Spring-loaded grabber (1974)

3 Tipper bucket (1974)

4 Cement mixer drum cone (1985)

5 Wrecking ball (2015)

BUILT FOR SPEED

If you've ever wanted to own a supercar, these LEGO® racing sets can make your dreams come true. But don't wait around: they disappear fast!

FACT STACK

The first LEGO racing set was Car with Trailer and Racer (set 650) in 1972.

The first minifigure racing driver came with Race Car (set 6609) in 1980.

More than 200 LEGO® Racers sets came out from 2001 to 2013.

REALLY?!

The LEGO® Power Racers Tow Trasher (set 8140) from 2007 is designed to fall apart – purely for dramatic effect!

LOOK CLOSER

The removable engine in 2015's 1,158-piece Ferrari F40 (set 10248) is made with eight antique pistol pieces as exhaust headers!

AWESOME!

The wheels on LEGO Speed Champions cars have realistic interchangeable hubcaps, not seen in any other theme.

FAST FACTS

Since 2015, the LEGO® Speed Champions theme has recreated real-life sports cars and racers with impressively realistic results, including...

... The Mopar Dodge//SRT Top Fuel Dragster from set 76904 – the longest Speed Champions car at 35 cm (14 in).

... The Ford Model A Hot Rod from set 75875 – the only vintage car in the theme.

KEY DATES

1998
Radio Control Racer (set 5600) becomes the first radio-control LEGO vehicle. It comes with instructions for five different racing cars.

2001
LEGO Racers sets screech into stores. They feature small cars with speed-demon driver pieces made especially for the theme.

2002
Racers step up a gear with larger sets, remote-control units, pullback motors, and drivers with minifigure heads on one-piece bodies.

2005
LEGO Power Racers mixes ramps, launchers, motors, fly-apart features and spinning obstacles to create an array of exciting stunt vehicles.

2010
LEGO® World Racers pitches minifigure team the X-treme Daredevils against the Backyard Blasters in racing cars, race bikes, race boats, and race snowmobiles!

IT'S A SIGN!

The Tiny Turbos subtheme of LEGO Racers features fun, fast cars made with the fewest pieces possible. They are still packed with details, though – as the tiny stickered logos on this Rally Sprinter (set 8120) show!

Brick History

In 1998, the LEGO Group produced its first Ferrari-themed set – Ferrari Formula 1 Racing Car (set 2556). Since then, there have been more than 50 Ferrari sets.

YOU'LL SEE ME ON THE PODIUM!

WOW!

Each LEGO Speed Champions car comes with a unique minifigure dressed in accurate gear for their real-life team.

... The 2018 MINI John Cooper Works Buggy – the first Speed Champions car with working suspension.

... The Formula E Panasonic Jaguar from set 76898 – the first Speed Champions set to be based on all-electric vehicles.

HEROIC RIDES AND VILLAINOUS VEHICLES

In the battle between LEGO® DC Comics Super Heroes and their criminal counterparts, victory depends on what vehicle you drive!

Wonder Woman's Invisible Jet is made using almost all transparent pieces.

THE CONTROLS ARE HARD TO READ.

AWESOME!

FACT STACK

The first LEGO DC Universe Super Heroes sets came out in 2012.

In 2014, the theme became LEGO DC Comics Super Heroes.

Between 2016 and 2018, Mighty Micros sets provided compact cars for LEGO DC stars.

GET YOUR SKATE ON

Who needs a Batmobile? All Batgirl needs to defeat the bad guys in 2021's Batman vs. The Joker: Batmobile Chase (set 76180) is a skateboard!

IT'S A SIGN!

The symbol on Green Lantern's spaceship (set 76025) is shaped like a green lamp: the insignia of intergalactic peacekeeping group the Green Lantern Corps.

FUN 5
Mighty Micros sets

1 Catwoman's Catmobile has ears and a tail!

2 The Flash drives a lightning-fast red racer.

3 Harley Quinn's car is a bit of a wind-up!

4 Superman's supercar flies along with outstretched arms.

Q Riddle me this: what's long, thin, fast, and green?

A A runner bean! Or the 2014's Riddler's Dragster from Batman: The Riddler Chase (set 76012).

LOOK CLOSER

The front of Brainiac's flying saucer in 2015's Brainiac Attack (set 76040) is a scary skull face!

SMILE FOR THE ROLLER!

Brick History

Two-Face was the first villain to get his own getaway car, in Batmobile and in 2012's Two-Face Chase (set 6864). Like him, it had a lighter side and a darker one!

5 **Bizarro's** car is Superman's built backwards!

REALLY?!

In 2014's Batman: The Penguin Face Off (set 76010), the bird-brained Penguin gets around in a giant rubber duck!

IT CAME WITH A BIG BILL!

BAT-VEHICLES

With a Batcave packed with crime-fighting cars and other hi-tech transport, Batman is always on the move in the LEGO® Batman and LEGO DC Super Heroes themes.

MOST COLOURFUL BAT-VEHICLE

Mighty Micros Batcopter (set 76069), 2017

I THOUGHT I'D BRIGHTEN UP THIS PAGE.

FACT STACK

The first LEGO Bat-vehicles hit the streets in 2006, in the LEGO Batman theme.

In 2012, LEGO Batman became part of the DC Super Heroes theme.

There are more than 40 different LEGO Batmobiles, including LEGO® DUPLO® and LEGO Technic versions.

FUN 5
LEGO Batmobiles

1 The first LEGO Batmobile (set 7781) has a massive missile in the front!

2 This Batmobile from 2018 (set 76112) can be remote-controlled with an app.

3 Though it came out in 2021, this Batmobile (set 76188) is straight out of the 1960s!

4 This big-wheeled Batmobile (set 76239) is also known as the Tumbler.

5 In 2022, this Batmobile (set 76181) was bursting with blue flames!

AWESOME!

In 2017's Knightcrawler Tunnel Attack (set 76086), Batman's armoured vehicle can move on wheels or on spider-like legs!

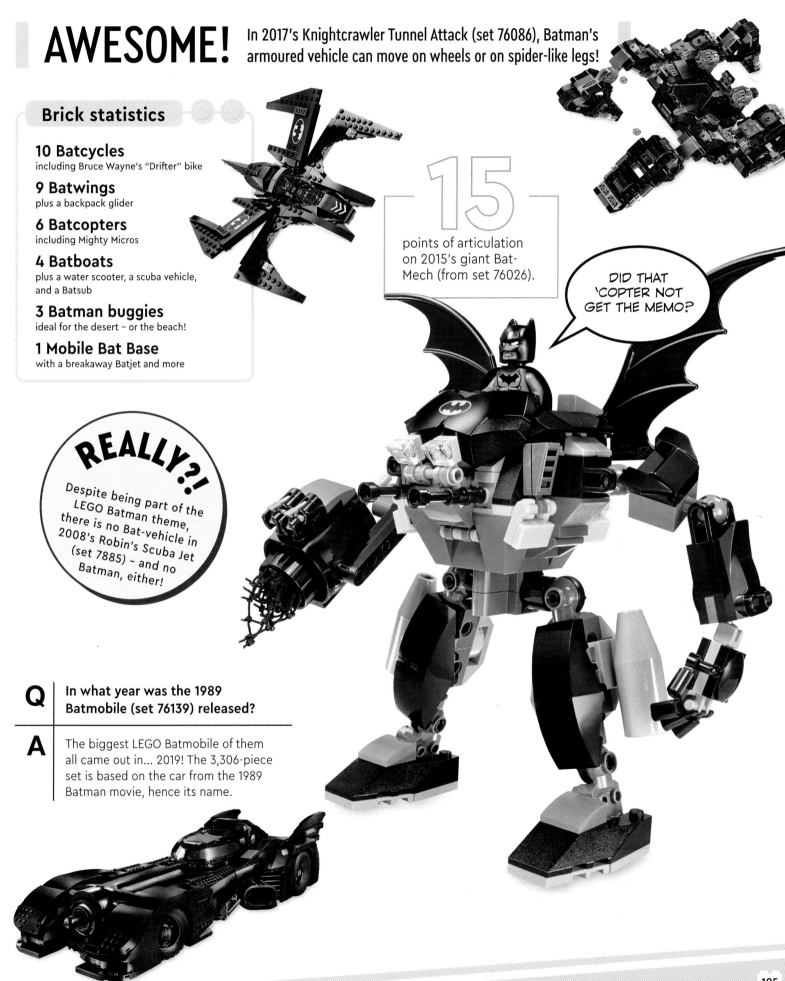

Brick statistics

10 Batcycles
including Bruce Wayne's "Drifter" bike

9 Batwings
plus a backpack glider

6 Batcopters
including Mighty Micros

4 Batboats
plus a water scooter, a scuba vehicle, and a Batsub

3 Batman buggies
ideal for the desert – or the beach!

1 Mobile Bat Base
with a breakaway Batjet and more

15

points of articulation on 2015's giant Bat-Mech (from set 76026).

DID THAT 'COPTER NOT GET THE MEMO?

REALLY?!

Despite being part of the LEGO Batman theme, there is no Bat-vehicle in 2008's Robin's Scuba Jet (set 7885) – and no Batman, either!

Q | In what year was the 1989 Batmobile (set 76139) released?

A | The biggest LEGO Batmobile of them all came out in... 2019! The 3,306-piece set is based on the car from the 1989 Batman movie, hence its name.

Famous four-wheelers from film and TV

1 From 2006 to 2012, the LEGO®
SpongeBob SquarePants™ theme
gave us inventive vehicles, including
the burger-shaped **Patty Wagon**, from
Krusty Krab Adventures (set 3833).

2 **The Mystery Machine** (set 75902)
from 2015 has room for cartoon canine
Scooby-Doo, two of his plucky pals,
and – of course – a giant sandwich
to snack on!

3 The *Ghostbusters* **Ecto-1** (set 75828)
from the 2016 movie has plenty of
room inside for all four ghoul-catching
heroes. It's based on a 1980 Cadillac
Hearse Wagon.

CARS

4   The **Back to the Future Time Machine** (set 10300) from 2022 can be built in three different ways, to match each of its three blockbuster appearances on the big screen.

5   **The Weasleys' Ford Anglia.** The Weasleys' flying family car appeared in two LEGO® *Harry Potter*™ sets: Escape from Privet Drive (set 4728) and Hogwarts Express (set 4841).

6   Released in 2022, the LEGO Speed Champions version of **James Bond's Aston Martin DB5** (set 76911) comes with swappable number plates and a stylish superspy minifigure!

BIG AND BOLD

Some of the biggest LEGO® vehicles are meant for display rather than play, but they still offer hours of building fun and plenty of interactive detail!

LARGE-SCALE RAIL

Part of the 1970s Hobby Set range, Thatcher Perkins Locomotive (set 396) is the only LEGO train engine larger than minifigure (or LEGO DUPLO figure) scale.

Piece particulars

The car door handles on the MINI Cooper (set 10242) from 2014 are more usually used as minifigure ice skates!

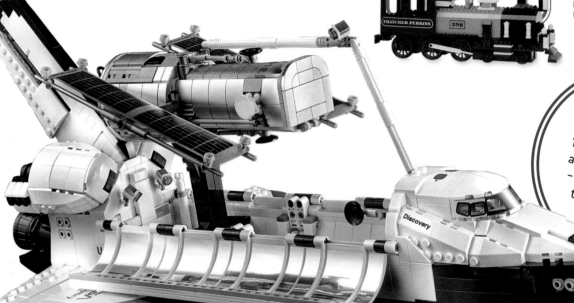

WOW!

Open up NASA Space Shuttle *Discovery* (set 10283), and you'll find a bumper build inside – a realistic model of the Hubble Space Telescope!

NASA ✦ esa
Hubble Space Telescope

Launch:	April 24, 1990
Launch Mass:	24,490 lbs
Velocity:	4.72 mi/s
Deploy Altitude:	350 miles

NASA
Space Shuttle Discovery STS-31

Wingspan:	78.06 ft
Launches:	39
Active:	August 30, 1984 – March 9, 2011
Orbital Velocity:	17,500 mi/h
Max Altitude:	350 miles
Earth Orbits:	5,830
Time in Space:	1 year, 22 hours, 39 minutes, 33 seconds

127

stickers are used to label all the cargo containers in 2014's huge cargo ship set, Maersk Line Triple-E (set 10241).

LOOK CLOSER

A surf scene in the homely interior of Volkswagen T1 Camper Van (set 10220) includes the initials of the set's designer, John-Henry Harris!

IT'S A SIGN!

Signage on the 1,686-piece London Bus (set 10258) from 2017 lists its destination as Brickston, via Yellow Brick Road and Brickadilly Circus!

Brick History

In 2003, Wright Flyer (set 10124) was released to mark the 100th anniversary of the first real-world-powered aeroplane. It has 670 pieces in just five colours.

FACT STACK

In the 1970s, LEGO® Hobby Set vehicles were among the first designed for play *and* display.

The LEGO® Model Team range was the home of large-scale vehicles in the 1980s and 1990s.

Today, the most challenging vehicles to build are part of the LEGO® Creator Expert theme.

cm (27 in) – the wingspan of the Boeing 787 Dreamliner (set 10177), the largest of any LEGO aircraft.

DOUBLE TAKE

The FIAT 500 is the only large-scale LEGO car to be released in two colours: cool yellow in 2020 (set 10271) and powder blue in 2021 (set 77942).

REALLY?!

The biggest set in the advanced LEGO Model Team range, Giant Truck (set 5571) has 1,757 pieces – including a cat for a bonnet ornament!

AWESOME!

FANTASTIC VOYAGERS

There's more to LEGO® vehicles than City cars and spaceships – just ask the drivers of these fantasy dream machines!

LOOK CLOSER

The LEGO® Hidden Side Phantom Fire Truck 3000 (set 70436) is decorated with stickers referencing LEGO® BIONICLE®, LEGO Town's Res-Q squad, and Rocket Racer (pictured) from 1999's LEGO® Racers videogame!

FACT STACK

Two themes have featured futuristic mining vehicles: LEGO® Rock Raiders in 1999, and LEGO® Power Miners in 2009.

In 2006, LEGO® EXO-FORCE™ was full of fantasy vehicles inspired by Japanese comics.

In 1996, the LEGO® Time Cruisers travelled in a Hypno Cruiser (set 6492) packed with historical hats!

95

animal-themed vehicles featured in LEGO® Legends of Chima™ sets between 2013 and 2015, including the sabre-toothed Tiger's Mobile Command (set 70224, pictured).

Brick statistics

LEGO EXO-FORCE Mobile Devastator (set 8108)

1,009 parts
including four giant, bright green wheels

60 cm (24 in) long
and 34 cm (13 in) tall

10 robot warriors on board
including robot leader Meca One

2 detachable robot scout ships
connected to the elevating battle tower

1 hero stands in its way
Ryo, in his *Blazing Falcon* battle machine!

KNIGHT MOVES

Between 2016 and 2018, the LEGO NEXO KNIGHTS theme mixed the medieval with the ultramodern to create a range of new fantasy vehicles. The Fortrex (set 70317), for example, was a castle that moved on caterpillar tracks!

NO MEDALS! CAN'T YOU SEE I'M UNDERCOVER?

MOST INAPPROPRIATELY NAMED VEHICLE

LEGO® Ultra Agents Stealth Patrol (set 70169)

WOW!

When battling the LEGO® Alpha Team, evil Ogel's Scorpion Orb Launcher (set 4774) can stand up on its mighty stinger to attack!

AWESOME!

In a world of hay carts and horses, Troll Battle Wheel (set 7041) is the most way-out weapon LEGO® Castle has ever seen!

IT'S A SIGN!

The printed face on the front of the LEGO® Monster Fighters Ghost Train (set 9467) looks even scarier when you see it glow in the dark!

STEPPING UP A GEAR

As well as looking incredible, the biggest LEGO®Technic vehicles are marvels of miniature engineering – and they keep on getting bigger with each passing year! Here are the biggest LEGO Technic vehicles so far...

1

4,108 PIECES

LIEBHERR R 9800

set number	42100
year released	2019
height	39 cm (15 in)
length	65 cm (25 in)
functions	App-programmable driving, boom, and bucket operation.

2

4,057 PIECES

ROUGH TERRAIN CRANE

set number	42082
year released	2018
height	100 cm (39 in)
length	76 cm (30 in)
functions	Motorized stabilizers, crane arm, and winch.

3

3,929 PIECES
BUCKET WHEEL EXCAVATOR

set number	42055
year released	2016
height	41 cm (16 in)
length	72 cm (28 in)
functions	Motorized caterpillar tracks, bucket wheel, and conveyor belts.

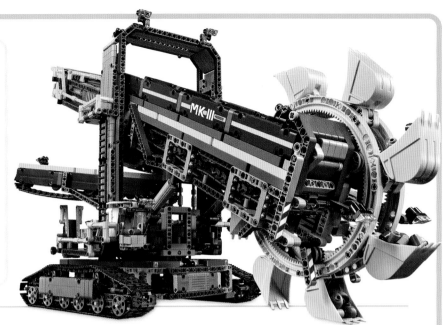

4

3,854 PIECES
CAT D11 BULLDOZER

set number	42131
year released	2021
height	26 cm (10 in)
length	57 cm (22 in)
functions	App-controlled tracks, blade, ripper, and ladder.

5

3,778 PIECES
FERRARI DAYTONA SP3

set number	42143
year released	2022
height	14 cm (5½ in)
length	59 cm (23 in)
functions	Steering, 8-speed sequential gearbox with paddle shifter

STATION TO STATION

LEGO® passenger trains have been getting LEGO citizens to where they need to go since... before there were LEGO citizens! Some are superfast, while others belong to the age of steam.

Brick History

In 1976, Western Train (set 726) was the first to carry passengers, in the form of three cowboy figures and a brick-built horse.

IT'S A SIGN!

DB 7715

In the 1980s, most LEGO trains came with sticker sheets featuring the logos of different national rail operators, so you could customize your train according to your country!

WOW!

Designed for use with the 1991 Metroliner (set 4558), Club Car (set 4547) from 1993 is the only double-decker LEGO® Trains set.

EMERALD NIGHT 10194

HI! DO YOU LIKE MY SHIRT?

FUN 5
First-class train travellers

1 **Classic Space Fan** aboard Holiday Train (set 60197), 2018

2 **Journalist** from High-Speed Passenger Train (set 60051), 2014

3 **Day Tripper** on Express Passenger Train (set 60337), 2022

4 **Tourist** from Passenger Train (set 7938), 2010

AWESOME!

The LEGOLAND® Train (set 4000014) is a very rare replica of a ride at LEGOLAND Billund. It was given away to a few lucky fans in 2014.

The LEGOLAND® Train

FACT STACK

The first LEGO System Train (set 323) was a 1964 push-along vehicle with no rails.

LEGO Trains without a power source are designed so that one can be added easily.

To date, there have been more than 30 passenger trains in a variety of LEGO themes.

DREAM DESIGNS

When 2009's awesome Emerald Night (set 10194) was being designed, the LEGO Group flew 10 fan builders to its head office in Denmark, then got them to describe their dream LEGO train.

REALLY?!

Passengers could drive their cars onto 1999's futuristic Railway Express (set 4561) before heading to the on-board pizza restaurant!

Piece particulars

The large grey switches that controlled 12-volt trains in the 1980s could also remotely operate lights, signals, points, level crossings, and even wagon separation.

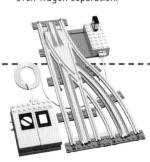

IT'S WHY I'M WEARING SHADES.

5 Definitely Not a Spy on the High-Speed Train (set 4511), 2003

7 speeds to choose from with 2014's superfast High-Speed Passenger Train (set 60051).

KEY DATES

1966
The first powered LEGO train features a 4.5-volt battery pack and special train wheels, and runs on new blue track pieces.

1969
Mains-powered LEGO trains driven by a 12-volt conductor rail and the first powered rail-switching points are introduced in Europe.

1980
A new look for LEGO Trains includes realistic grey tracks and a revamped 12-volt system offering a wealth of remote-control functions.

1991
A single 9-volt mains-powered system replaces both 4.5-volt battery power and 12-volt mains power as the standard for LEGO Trains.

2006
The LEGO Trains theme is integrated into LEGO City, and a new infrared remote-control system powered by rechargeable batteries is launched.

2010
The first of several LEGO City trains designed specifically for use with a battery-operated LEGO Power Functions motor is released.

Goods carried by classic LEGO® cargo trains

CARGO

1   Farm animals

The 2014 Cargo Train (set 60052) has a spacious cattle truck, plus room for a fuel tank, a forklift, and two giant cable drums!

2   Heavy machinery

The 1980 Diesel Freight Train (set 7720) could carry cargo loaded onto it by a digger – as well as the digger itself!

3   Other vehicles

In service since 2022, Freight Train (set 60336) not only carries two electric cars, but also a solar-charging station to power them!

4   Valuables

Classic Train (set 3225) from 1998 has a fragile crate of glasses amid its cargo, and a $100 note hidden among the mail!

5   Building materials

In 1996, Freight and Crane Railway (set 4565) came with a working scale for weighing cargo, which included two cement mixers!

6   Chilled goods

The 1,237-piece Maersk Train (set 10219) from 2011 is loaded with three huge cargo containers, including one refrigerator container.

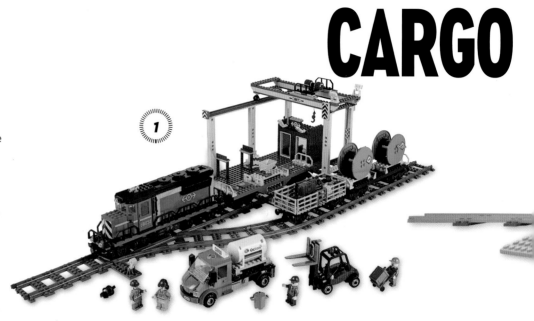

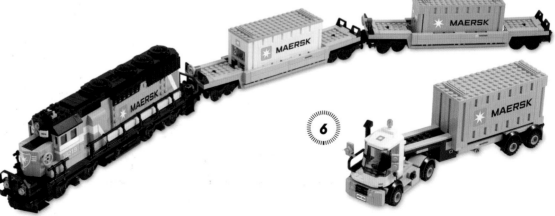

A-GO-GO!

2

5

Plus extra special deliveries...

Gold bars on 2003's Cargo Train (set 4512)

LEGO sets on 2010's Cargo Train (set 7939)

Elephants on 2005's LEGO DUPLO My First Train (set 3770)

Helicopters on 2015's Heavy-Haul Train (set 60098)

Lots of toys on 2006's Holiday Train (set 10173, pictured)

Christmas trees on 2016's Winter Holiday Train (set 10254)

SET SAIL!

There are enough LEGO® boats and ships to fill an ocean – well, at least a couple of bathtubs! Some of them float, while others are designed to look sunken.

2,741

Number of pieces in MetalBeard's Sea Cow (set 70810) from **THE LEGO® MOVIE™**.

AWESOME! The 2015 LEGO City Deep Sea Exploration Vessel (set 60095) comes with a shipwreck that collapses when you pull a hidden lever!

FACT STACK

In 1966, Master Mechanic (set 003) featured a moving, motorized Viking ship!

The first ship to be piloted by a minifigure was Police Boat (set 709) in 1978.

LEGO DUPLO ships include a glow-in-the-dark Pirate Ship (set 7881) from 2006!

Piece particulars

Some LEGO vessels can float using special watertight hull pieces. The first was Tugboat (set 310), released in 1973.

OCEANS APART

The LEGO Technic Ocean Explorer (set 42064) from 2017 has a whopping 1,327 pieces. The LEGO Creator Ocean Explorer (set 31045) from 2016 packs all its details into just 213!

REALLY?!

The 2020 LEGO Friends Party Boat (set 41433) includes a second craft in the shape of a giant flamingo!

LOOK CLOSER

In 2019's Dragon Boat Race (set 80103), one dragon head has a croissant piece for a snout, while the other one uses an old-fashioned telephone receiver piece!

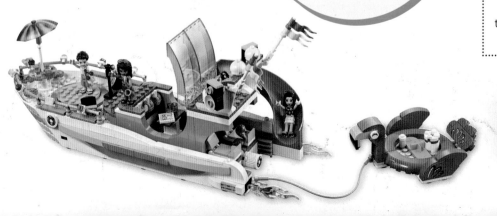

FUN 5

Fanta-sea ships

1 LEGO Castle Troll Warship (set 7048), 2008

2 LEGO Legends of Chima Cragger's Command Ship (set 70006), 2013

3 LEGO® Elves Naida's Epic Adventure Ship (set 41073), 2015

4 LEGO Ultra Agents Ocean HQ (set 70173), 2015

5 LEGO® NINJAGO® *Destiny's Bounty* (set 71705), 2020

Q Can you fit a LEGO ship inside a bottle?

A You can if the bottle is made from LEGO elements as well! That's the secret behind the LEGO® Ideas Ship in a Bottle (set 21313) from 2018.

Brick History

In 2016, LEGO® Education released a 1,184-piece working model of The Panama Canal (set 2000451), with four adjustable locks and five model ships.

WOW!

The LEGO City Speedboat (set 7244) from 2005 doesn't just float on water – it zooms along it using a battery-powered motor!

UP, UP AND AWAY

These true-to-life aircraft are packed so full of play features, it's a wonder they ever get off the ground!

WOW!

Aerial Defence Unit (set 8971) is a LEGO® Agents helicopter from 2009. Its trigger-activated twin propellers overlap, but amazingly never collide.

PLANE PACKAGING

LEGO DUPLO Airplane (set 5504) was released in 2005. It comprises 30 standard LEGO DUPLO bricks in a special aeroplane-shaped container.

Brick History

In 2016, the LEGO City Volcano Exploration Base (set 60124) was the first set to feature an unmanned aerial vehicle (drone) in a realistic setting.

LOOK CLOSER

The goods being transported by plane in 2013's Cargo Terminal (set 60022) include two brick-sized LEGO sets – including the LEGO City sets in distinctive blue packaging.

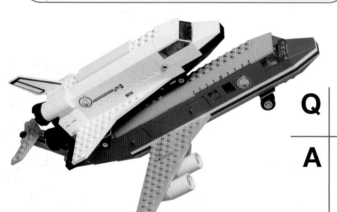

Q | Why is there a set with a spaceship on top of a plane?

A | Until 2012, jumbo jets really were used to transport space shuttles around the US. This was the inspiration for the 1995 LEGO Town set Shuttle Transcon 2 (set 6544).

FUN 5
Heavy-duty helicopters

1 Light & Sound Rescue Helicopter (set 6482)

2 Fire Helicopter (set 7206)

3 Coast Guard Helicopter (set 60013)

4 Jungle Air Drop Helicopter (set 60161)

5 Arctic Air Transport (set 60193)

FACT STACK

The first aircraft-themed LEGO set was the 79-piece Aeroplanes (set 311), which flew into stores in 1961.

Minifigures first flew in 1978's Coast Guard Station (set 575), a US-only release.

There were two planes in the LEGO® Fabuland theme. Both of them were flown by birds!

REALLY?!

The biplane in the LEGO City Airport Air Show (set 60103) from 2016 has a platform on top for a daredevil wing-walker!

MAKE WAY FOR WING-WALKERS!

YIKES!

The first LEGO City hot-air balloon was used by crooks fleeing Prison Island (set 60130) in 2016!

5

pieces used to make each aeroplane in 2014's Billund Airport (set 4000016).

SKY-HIGH SALES

Several aircraft sets have been made specially for sale on airlines. Holiday Jet (set 4032) from 2003 came with different logo decorations depending on which airline you were travelling with.

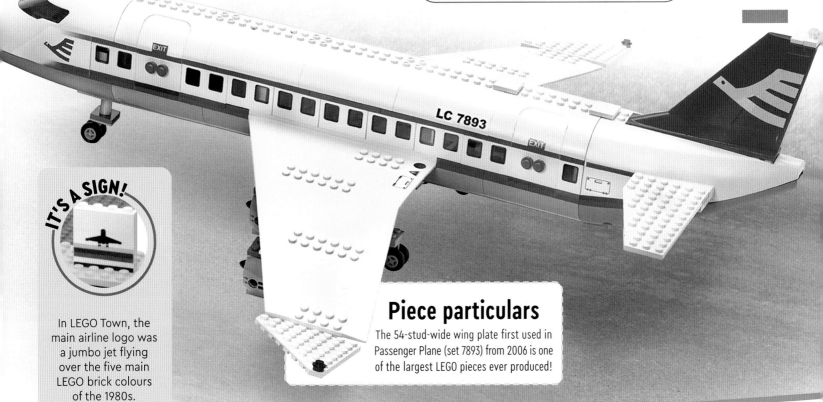

LC 7893

IT'S A SIGN!

In LEGO Town, the main airline logo was a jumbo jet flying over the five main LEGO brick colours of the 1980s.

Piece particulars

The 54-stud-wide wing plate first used in Passenger Plane (set 7893) from 2006 is one of the largest LEGO pieces ever produced!

MY BUSINESS IS REALLY TAKING OFF!

High-flying fantasy vehicles soar above many LEGO® worlds...

1 This aeroplane from THE LEGO MOVIE *Creative Ambush* (set 70812) was a kebab stand before it was rebuilt during the battle against Lord Business.

2 She may have a perfectly good broomstick, but the magical minifigure in LEGO Castle's *Witch's Windship* (set 6037) prefers to fly using dragon power!

3 Cragger's Fire Helicroctor comes from the LEGO Legends of Chima set *King Crominus' Rescue* (set 70227). It's ideal if you need to be somewhere in a snap!

4 Aimed squarely at attacking lava monsters, *Aaron Fox's Aero-Striker V2* (set 70320) from LEGO® NEXO KNIGHTS™ is a giant, sky-slicing crossbow.

5 Part pirate ship, part aeroplane, and possibly even part dragon, the LEGO® Time Cruisers *Flying Time Vessel* (set 6493) would look strange in any era!

6 The LEGO® Adventurers *Expedition Balloon* (set 5956) is the only set ever to feature this immense airship piece.

THE LIMIT

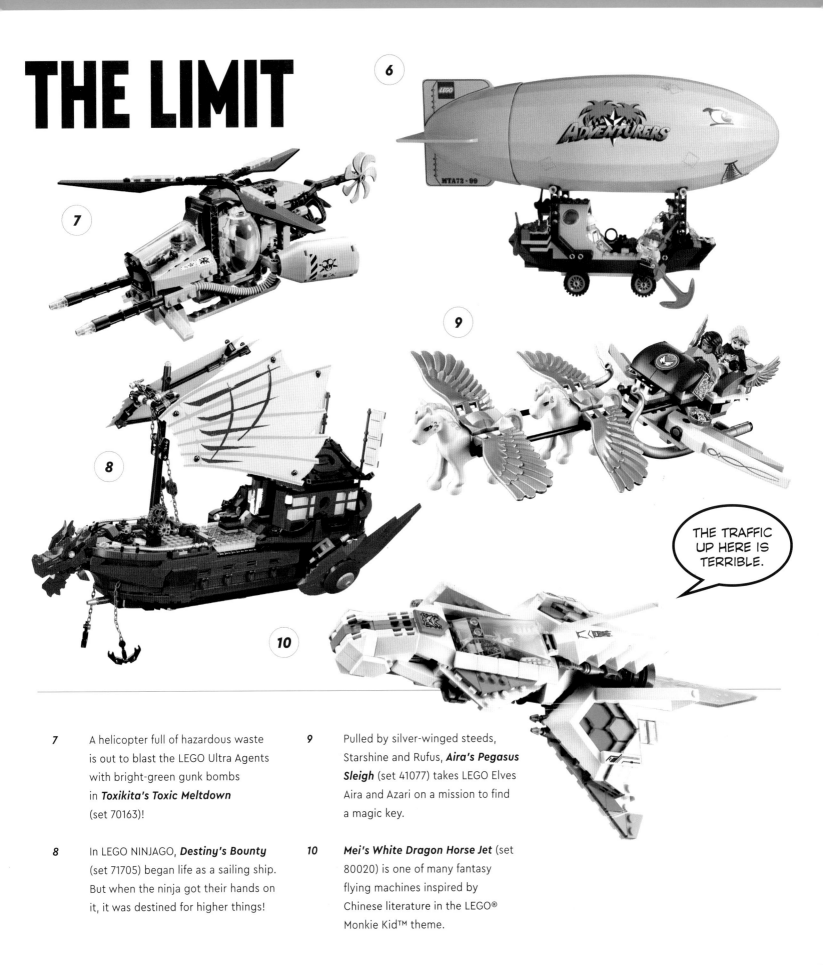

THE TRAFFIC UP HERE IS TERRIBLE.

7   A helicopter full of hazardous waste is out to blast the LEGO Ultra Agents with bright-green gunk bombs in **Toxikita's Toxic Meltdown** (set 70163)!

8   In LEGO NINJAGO, **Destiny's Bounty** (set 71705) began life as a sailing ship. But when the ninja got their hands on it, it was destined for higher things!

9   Pulled by silver-winged steeds, Starshine and Rufus, **Aira's Pegasus Sleigh** (set 41077) takes LEGO Elves Aira and Azari on a mission to find a magic key.

10 **Mei's White Dragon Horse Jet** (set 80020) is one of many fantasy flying machines inspired by Chinese literature in the LEGO® Monkie Kid™ theme.

NINJA, GO!

No one can call on as many cool vehicles as a NINJAGO ninja – except, perhaps, their enemies! From concept cars to combo mechs, a ninja's journey never ends...

4

vehicles combine to build 2022's awesome Ninja Ultra Combo Mech (set 71765).

Brick History

Back in 2011, the first foes faced by the ninja were members of the Skeleton Army. Their vehicles were all bad to the bone – like the skull-shaped helicopter in Lightning Dragon Battle (set 2521)!

FACT STACK

More than 200 vehicles have featured in the LEGO NINJAGO theme since 2011.

No mechs appeared in the first year of the theme – but there has been at least one every year since!

There have been five versions of the ninja's ship, *Destiny's Bounty*, including one from THE LEGO® NINJAGO MOVIE™.

WOW!

The biggest bad guy vehicle faced by the ninja is the Dragon Hunter's Dieselnaut (set 70654) from 2018. At 1,179 pieces, it is one piece bigger than the Land Bounty!

REALLY?!

In 2012, the ninja did battle with the Fangpyre Wrecking Ball (set 9457) – a massive mechanical snake designed for demolition!

AWESOME!

Ninja of Fire Kai can't get enough of motorbikes. He even has one built into his 2021 car, the X-1 Ninja Charger (set 71737)!

Q Is *Destiny's Bounty* the ninja's only mobile base?

A No – the flying ship shares HQ duties with sleek submarine the Hydro Bounty (set 71756), hi-tech truck the Ninja DB X (set 70750), and awesome off-roader the Land Bounty (set 70677, pictured).

LOOK CLOSER

The smooth sides of the ninja's 2017 boat, *Destiny's Shadow* (set 70623), are made from canoe pieces first seen in LEGO® Pirates sets back in 1994.

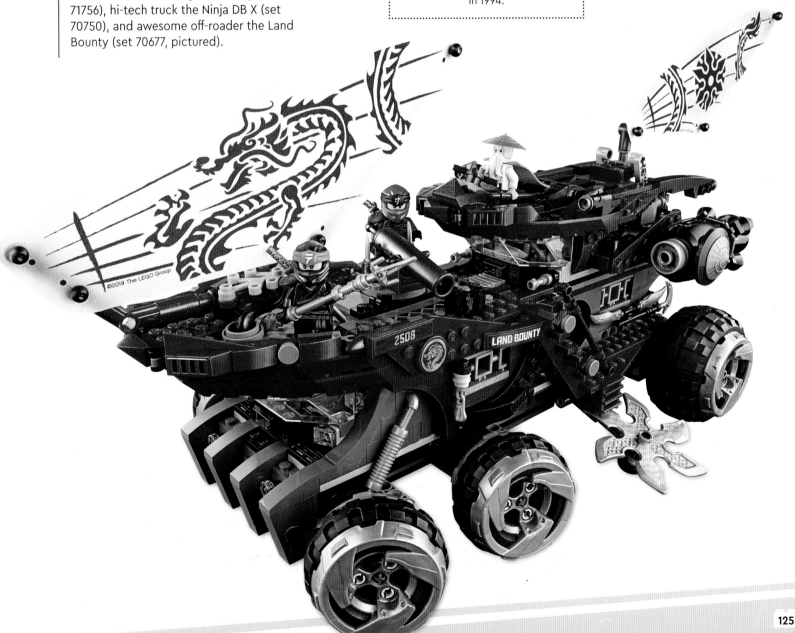

©2019 The LEGO Group

2508

LAND BOUNTY

MONKIE ON THE MOVE

Blending the modern and the mythical, LEGO® Monkie Kid™ is packed full of inventive vehicles, from triple-decker trucks to monstrous mechs!

FUN 5

Vehicles made from Monkie Kid's team

1 Racing car

2 Jet flyer

3 Cloud flyer

4 Submarine

5 Mech

8

rollercoaster track pieces are used to make the giant spinning wheel of Nezha's Fire Ring (set 80034) from 2022.

ONE SMALL HOP...

Rabbits play many roles in Chinese mythology, but Chang'e Moon Cake Factory (set 80032) might just be the first time they've piloted a carrot-powered mech on the moon!

REALLY?!

Sandy's Power Loader Mech (set 80025) has a built-in DJ platform, where Mo the cat can scratch the records in between a pair of orange speakers!

DISH OF THE DAY

Pigsy's Noodle Tank (set 80026), 2021

WOW!

Monkie Kid's Team Van (set 80038) is a triple-decker treasure trove – opening to reveal a go-kart, an arcade game, a basketball hoop, and a table tennis table!

AWESOME!

Animal mechs in the Monkie Kid theme include giant monkeys, bulls, and lions, as well as the eight-legged Spider Queen's Arachnoid Base (set 80022)!

BIG STEPS FOR MECHS

Mechs have walked the LEGO® world for many years. The fantasy machine suits with minifigure pilots inside come in all shapes and sizes, and are always advancing in great strides!

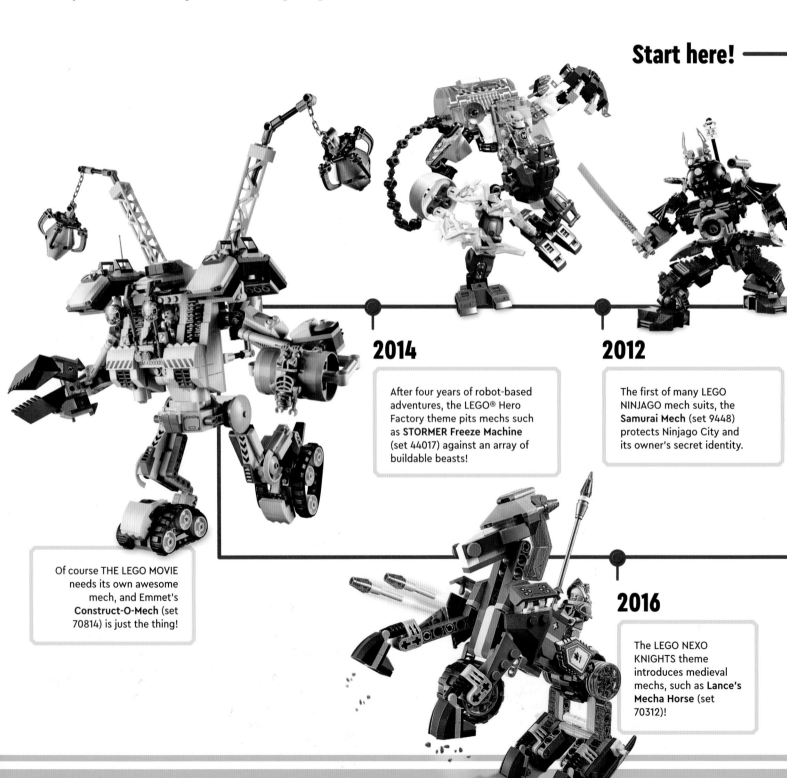

Start here!

2014

After four years of robot-based adventures, the LEGO® Hero Factory theme pits mechs such as **STORMER Freeze Machine** (set 44017) against an array of buildable beasts!

2012

The first of many LEGO NINJAGO mech suits, the **Samurai Mech** (set 9448) protects Ninjago City and its owner's secret identity.

Of course THE LEGO MOVIE needs its own awesome mech, and Emmet's **Construct-O-Mech** (set 70814) is just the thing!

2016

The LEGO NEXO KNIGHTS theme introduces medieval mechs, such as **Lance's Mecha Horse** (set 70312)!

One of the first LEGO mechs, the LEGO® Space Futuron **Strategic Pursuer** (set 6848) allows its solo pilot to safely carry out scientific research on distant planets.

1988

2001

When LEGO Space explorers discover life on Mars, they also find cool Martian tech, such as the **Recon Mech RP** (set 7314).

2006

Inspired by hi-tech mechs in Japanese manga, the LEGO EXO-FORCE theme centres around mighty mech battles. The **Grand Titan** (set 7701) stands over 19 cm (7½ in) tall.

2010

The **Magma Mech** (set 8189) is kitted out with everything the LEGO Power Miners need to battle red-hot Lava Monsters, including a spiralled drill piece and grabbing claw.

Mechs walk underwater in LEGO® Atlantis sets in 2010. The **Undersea Explorer** (set 8080) transforms from a six-wheeled rover into a mighty mech!

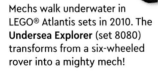

2018

The biggest LEGO mech of them all, the **LEGO Ideas Voltron** (set 21311), is made from 2,321 pieces!

2020

The LEGO Monkie Kid theme brings a majestic new look to LEGO mechs such as the **Monkey King Warrior Mech** (set 80012).

TO THE MOON AND BACK

As well as the science fiction of the LEGO® Space theme, many LEGO sets have explored the science fact of space exploration – starting way back before the first moon landing!

SETS IN SPACE

In 2011, NASA sent 14 LEGO sets to the International Space Station (ISS), which the astronauts built while orbiting Earth. Nine years later, the ISS became an official LEGO Ideas set (set 21321)!

Piece particulars

To help set up their cameras in Martian daylight, NASA fitted red, blue, and yellow "LEGO plates" to its Mars rovers in 2003. These plates were actually custom-made metal pieces, designed to look like LEGO elements.

RED ROVER GOES TO MARS

HELLO!

Q Have any real-life NASA astronauts been made into minifigures?

A Yes – both Sally Ride and Mae Jemison appear in 2017's Women of NASA (set 21312), alongside astronomer Nancy Grace Roman and computer scientist Margaret Hamilton.

Mae Jemison   Sally Ride

KEY DATES

1973
A year after astronauts last walked on the moon, Rocket Base (set 358) features a realistic rocket, complete with command module.

1995
LEGO Town starts the Launch Command space programme – its own friendly rival to NASA!

2003
The LEGO Group partners with Discovery Channel for six space sets, including a Lunar Lander (set 10029) with two Apollo astronauts.

2015
LEGO City gets a brand-new spaceport, plus a Training Jet Transporter (set 60079) for future shuttle pilots!

FACT STACK

The first outer space LEGO set was a 115-piece rocket in 1964.

The first LEGO space shuttle took off from LEGO Town in 1990.

More than 60 LEGO sets have had a real-world space theme.

The first moon landing was in 1969, so 2017's LEGO Ideas Apollo 11 Saturn V Rocket (set 21309) is built with 1,969 pieces!

FIRST LEGO FRIENDS IN SPACE

Olivia and William in Olivia's Space Academy (set 41713), 2022

I HOPE I DON'T HAVE HELMET HAIR.

Brick History

In 1975, Space Module with Astronauts (set 367) replicated a Moon landing with three brick-built spacemen, whose helmets could be swapped for faces.

Brick statistics

LEGO Technic Space Shuttle (set 8480), 1996

1,366 pieces
including a 9-volt motor

6 fibre-optic cables
for lighting the engine exhausts

2 motorized bay doors
built with angled beam pieces – new for 1996!

1 working crane arm
for launching the on-board satellite

8,536,186

kilometres (5,304,140 miles) travelled by a LEGO model of the space shuttle *Discovery* in 2010, while on board the real NASA space shuttle *Discovery*.

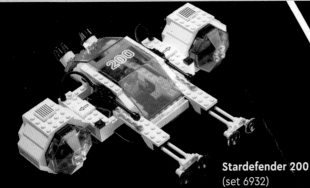

Stardefender 200
(set 6932)

A HISTORY OF THE FUTURE

LEGO® Space has changed a lot over the years, but one thing ties all the eras together, and that's spaceships, spaceships, SPACESHIPS!

Galactic Peace Keeper (set 6886)

1980s

New-look white exploration vessels continue to research the universe, while Space Police ships are on patrol for notorious Blacktron crooks.

1990s

Flying saucers and alien insects are just some of the strange sights to be spotted deeper into space.

Xenon X-Craft
(set 6872)

Insectoid Sonic Stinger (set 6907)

Space Dart I
(set 6824)

Space Transporter
(set 924)

1970s

The first LEGO astronauts blast off in blue and grey ships that don't stray too far from scientific fact.

Space Scooter
(set 885)

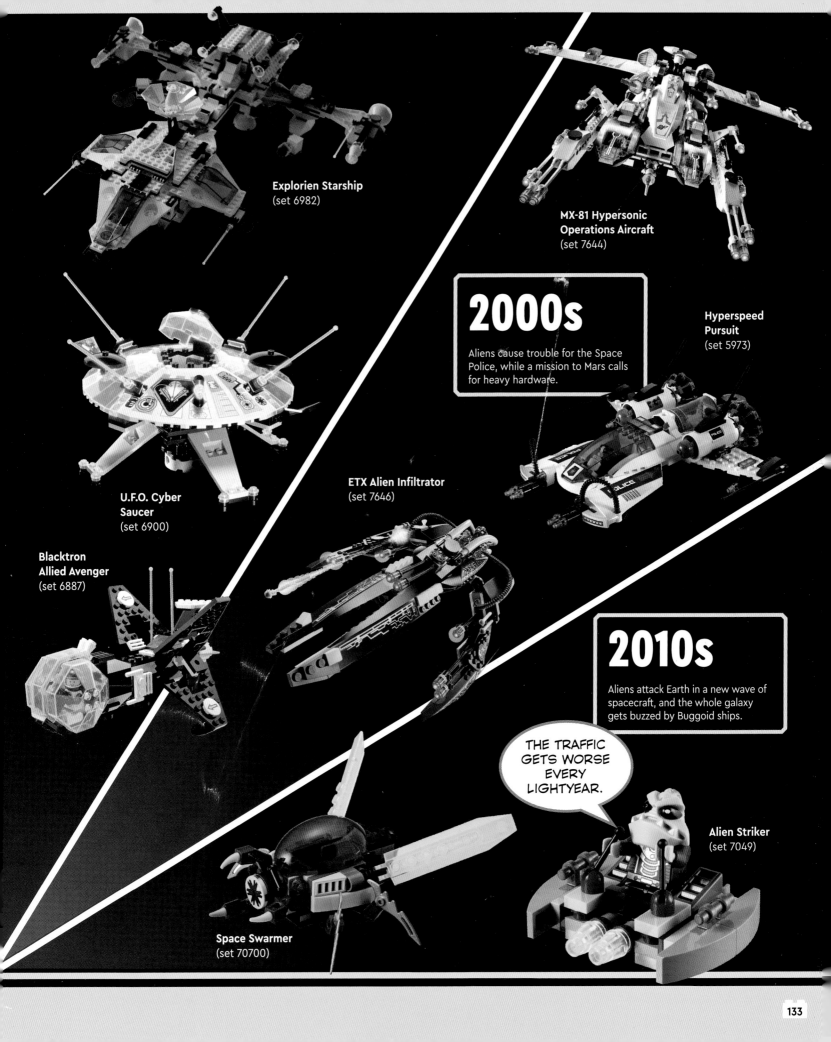

Explorien Starship
(set 6982)

**MX-81 Hypersonic
Operations Aircraft**
(set 7644)

2000s

Aliens cause trouble for the Space
Police, while a mission to Mars calls
for heavy hardware.

**Hyperspeed
Pursuit**
(set 5973)

**U.F.O. Cyber
Saucer**
(set 6900)

ETX Alien Infiltrator
(set 7646)

**Blacktron
Allied Avenger**
(set 6887)

2010s

Aliens attack Earth in a new wave of
spacecraft, and the whole galaxy
gets buzzed by Buggoid ships.

THE TRAFFIC
GETS WORSE
EVERY
LIGHTYEAR.

Alien Striker
(set 7049)

Space Swarmer
(set 70700)

PARKING SPACE

Spaceships aren't the only way to get around the galaxy! With wheels and walkers, LEGO® astronauts have charted many strange new worlds...

I'M WHEELY AWESOME.

12

wheels on the giant Roboforce Robomaster (set 2154) from 1997.

REALLY?!

The biggest LEGO Space ground vehicle, 2013's Galactic Titan (set 70709), has giant caterpillar tracks for going into battle with huge alien caterpillars!

FACT STACK

Moon buggies feature in all four of the first LEGO Space sets in 1978.

In total, more than 100 LEGO Space sets feature wheels.

Tripod Invader (set 7051) from 2011 is the only LEGO Space walker with three legs.

LOST IN SPACE

This six-wheeled satellite launcher was designed in the 1980s but never released. A single prototype box is kept securely in the LEGO Group archives.

FUN 5
Robotic rides

1 Robot Command Centre (set 6951), 1984

2 Alien Moon Stalker (set 6940), 1986

3 Spyrius Robo Guardian (set 6949), 1994

4 Life on Mars Recon Mech (set 7314), 2001

5 Galaxy Squad Star Slicer (set 70703), 2013

AWESOME!

The centrepiece of the LEGO Space theme in 1987 was the battery-powered Monorail Transport System (set 6990), a space train with more than 3 m (10 ft) of track!

6990

LEGOLAND

LEGO

Brick History

In 1985, Solar Power Transporter (set 6952) was the first LEGO Space convertible ground vehicle – transforming into two spaceships and a mobile base!

AM I AT THE FRONT OR THE BACK?

IT'S A SIGN!

7649

The muscular mutt design on the side of 2008's Mars Mission MT-201 Ultra-Drill Walker (set 7649) is based on LEGO designer Mark Stafford's own pet dog at the time.

GET ME TO A GALAXY FAR, FAR AWAY!

The LEGO® *Star Wars*™ theme has been flying high for nearly 25 years, and these are just some of the starships that have taken it to new heights.

386
black pieces in Krennic's Imperial Shuttle (set 75156).

FACT STACK

The first LEGO *Star Wars* starships launched in 1999.

More than 250 LEGO *Star Wars* starships have been released to date.

There have been starships based on movies, TV shows, games, and more!

Piece particulars
Not all LEGO *Star Wars* flying machines are futuristic! Wicket the Ewok flies a glider made with fishing rod pieces in 2009's The Battle of Endor (set 8038).

Brick statistics

26 TIE fighters
released at minifigure scale, including TIE Interceptors and other variants

11 X-wing fighters
at minifigure scale, including Poe Dameron's Black One

8 *Millennium Falcons*
at minifigure scale, including two Ultimate Collector Series sets

5 Lambda-class Imperial Shuttles
at minifigure scale, including one Ultimate Collector Series set

GETTING FROM A TO Y

Lots of *Star Wars* ships are named for their resemblance to letters, and every single one has been spelled out in LEGO bricks.

B IS FOR...
B-Wing (set 75050)

A IS FOR...
A-Wing (set 75175)

U IS FOR...
U-Wing (set 75155)

1 Han Solo's Millennium Falcon (set 75295), 2022

2 Ani Skywalker's Naboo Starfighter (set 75223), 2019

3 Kylo Ren's Shuttle (set 75264), 2020

4 Hera Syndulla's The Ghost (set 75127), 2016

5 The Mandalorian's Razor Crest (set 75321), 2022

AWESOME!

The LEGO *Star Wars Rebels* Wookiee Gunship (set 75084) from 2015 is the first Wookiee starship and the first set to feature rapid-fire stud shooters.

WOW!

The 2019 version of Princess Leia's *Tantive IV* (set 75244) is the largest LEGO *Star Wars* ship outside the Ultimate Collector Series.

REALLY?!

Luke Skywalker's X-Wing Fighter (set 4502) from 2004 comes covered in Dagobah swamp gunk!

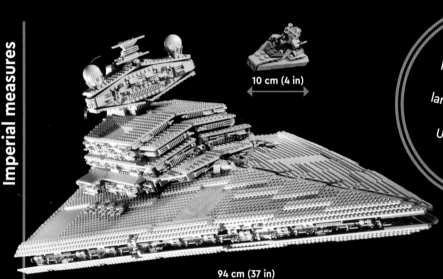

Imperial measures

10 cm (4 in)

94 cm (37 in)

Imperial Star Destroyer Ultimate Collector version (set 10030) 3,104 pieces, 94 cm (37 in) long

Imperial Star Destroyer Microfighter version (set 75033) 97 pieces, 10 cm (4 in) long

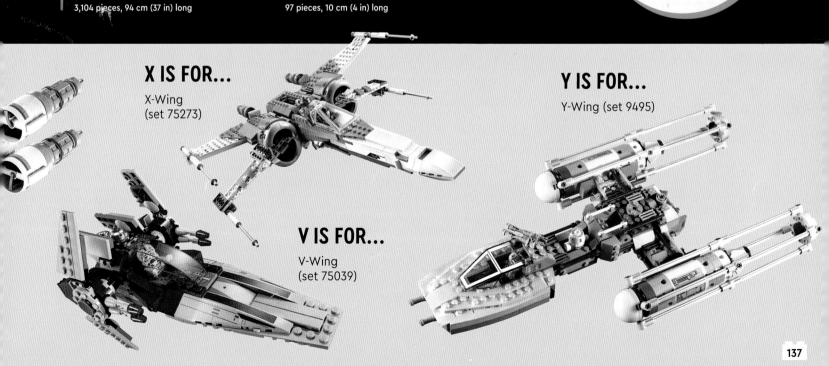

X IS FOR...
X-Wing (set 75273)

Y IS FOR...
Y-Wing (set 9495)

V IS FOR...
V-Wing (set 75039)

GROUND WARS

The LEGO® *Star Wars™* saga stretches across more than just space! There are worlds of sand, snow, forest, and fire, each needing special ways to get across its surface...

Brick History

LEGO *Star Wars* got its first train in 2018! The Imperial Conveyex Transport (set 75217) was one of several sets based on the adventures of young Han Solo.

Q Why are LEGO *Star Wars* walkers always grey? I want a colourful one!

A They aren't *always* grey! Check out 2019's AT-ST Raider (set 75254), which has been given a stripy makeover by Klatooinian Raiders!

WAY TO GO!

There are almost as many ways to get around a planet as there are planets to get around! All you need to do is pick a mode of propulsion...

TRACK POWER

Half tank, half droid, the Corporate Alliance Tank Droid (set 75015) from 2013 crawls along on a single caterpillar track.

LEG POWER

Captain Rex's AT-TE (set 75157) from 2016 has been modified from a walking weapon into a home.

FACT STACK

The LEGO *Star Wars* theme hit the ground in 1999 with 13 sets.

All but two of the first sets featured some kind of surface transport.

There are more than 25 different designs of LEGO *Star Wars* speeder bike!

15 pieces used to make Luke Skywalker's landspeeder in the 2014 LEGO *Star Wars* Advent Calendar. (The Ultimate Collector Series version has 1,890!)

BEST UNICYCLIST

General Grievous on his Wheel Bike (set 75040), 2014

REALLY?!

TIE fighters aren't only found in the sky! The TIE Crawler (set 7664) from 2007 runs on caterpillar tracks!

WHEEL POWER

The 10-wheeled Clone Turbo Tank (set 8098) from 2010 has more wheels than any other LEGO *Star Wars* vehicle, plus working suspension.

I'M JUST ONE DAY AWAY FROM RE-TYRING!

POD POWER

Anakin Skywalker's homemade Podracer (set 7962) from 2011 is nearly all engine, with just a small seat for a pilot pulled along behind.

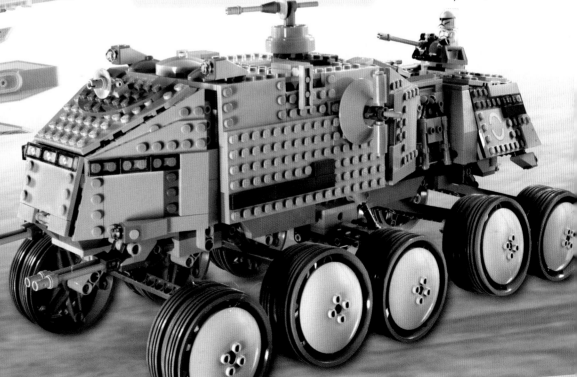

ULTRA COOL SETS

Unbelievably Complex Starships? Utterly Convincing Sculptures? In the LEGO® *Star Wars*™ theme, UCS stands for Ultimate Collector Series – some of the most advanced LEGO sets in the galaxy!

The series launches with a 703-piece **TIE Interceptor** (set 7181) and a 1,304-piece **X-wing Fighter** (set 7191).

2000

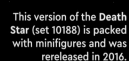

Start here!

This version of the **Death Star** (set 10188) is packed with minifigures and was rereleased in 2016.

2008

2010

Imperial Shuttle (set 10212) can be displayed with its wings open for flight or closed for landing.

2012

The UCS **R2-D2** (set 10225) is more than 200 times bigger than a minifigure-scale Artoo!

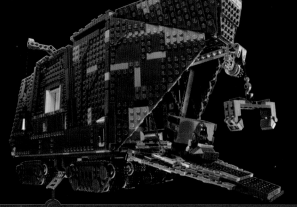

The first UCS **Snowspeeder** came out in 2003. This one (set 75144) adds more details – and minifigures!

2017

2014

The **Sandcrawler** (set 75059) features working cranes and steering, plus eight opening sections.

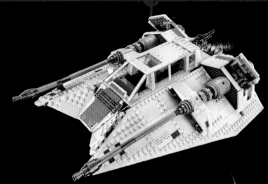

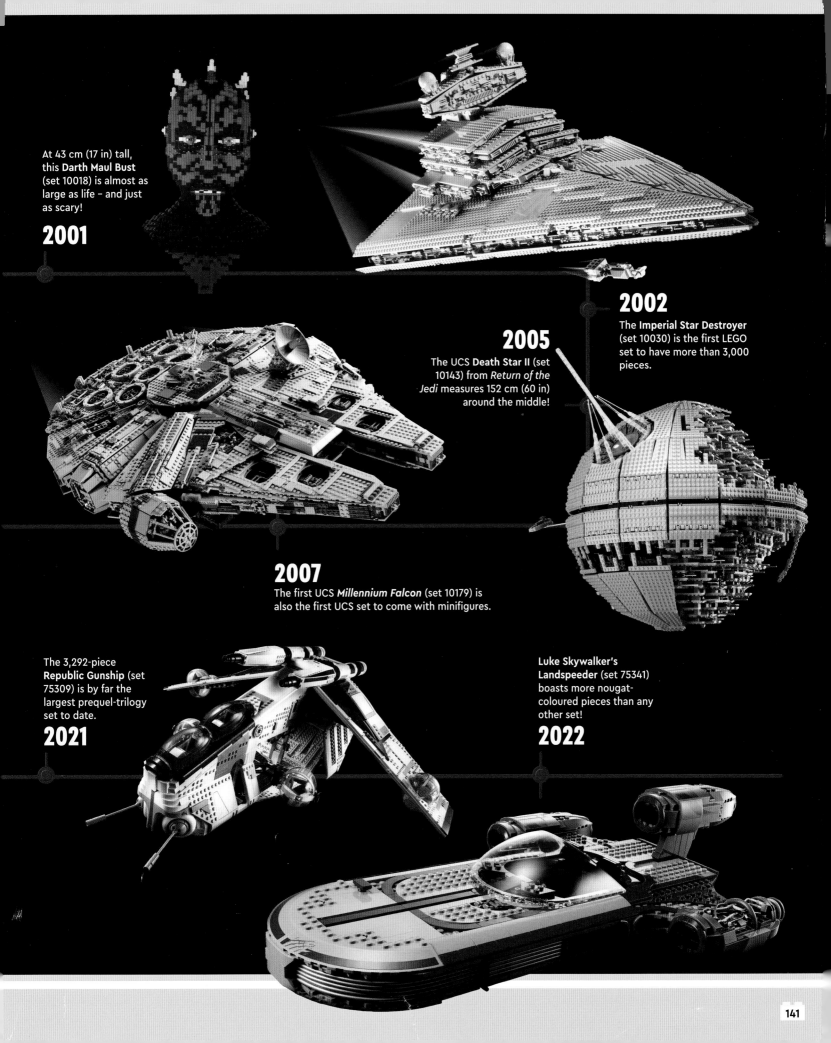

At 43 cm (17 in) tall, this **Darth Maul Bust** (set 10018) is almost as large as life – and just as scary!

2001

2002

The **Imperial Star Destroyer** (set 10030) is the first LEGO set to have more than 3,000 pieces.

2005

The UCS **Death Star II** (set 10143) from *Return of the Jedi* measures 152 cm (60 in) around the middle!

2007

The first UCS *Millennium Falcon* (set 10179) is also the first UCS set to come with minifigures.

The 3,292-piece **Republic Gunship** (set 75309) is by far the largest prequel-trilogy set to date.

2021

Luke Skywalker's **Landspeeder** (set 75341) boasts more nougat-coloured pieces than any other set!

2022

THE WORLD'S BIGGEST LEGO® VEHICLE: X-WING STARFIGHTER

On 23 May 2013, the LEGO Group unveiled a life-sized LEGO *Star Wars* X-Wing Starfighter in New York's Times Square.

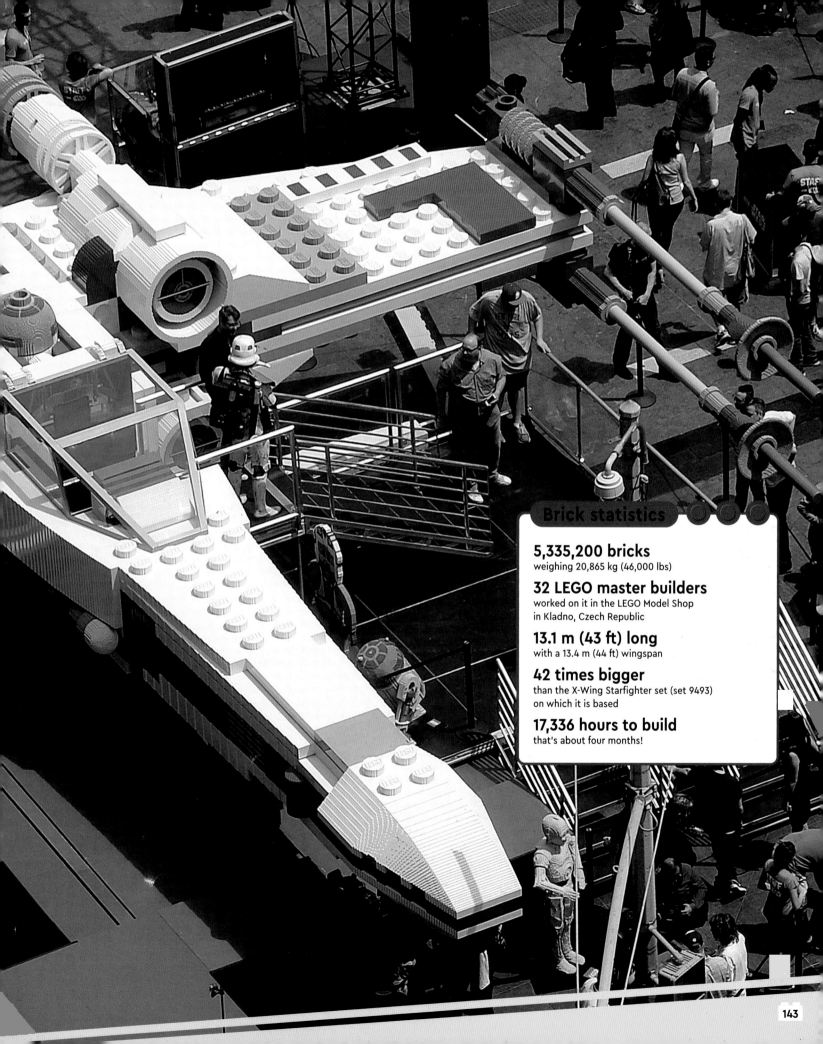

Brick statistics

5,335,200 bricks
weighing 20,865 kg (46,000 lbs)

32 LEGO master builders
worked on it in the LEGO Model Shop
in Kladno, Czech Republic

13.1 m (43 ft) long
with a 13.4 m (44 ft) wingspan

42 times bigger
than the X-Wing Starfighter set (set 9493)
on which it is based

17,336 hours to build
that's about four months!

CHAPTER FOUR

MINIFIGURES, MONSTERS, AND MORE

SMALL BEGINNINGS

In 1978, the first minifigures added new character to the worlds of LEGO® sets. Their insistent smiles and ingenious design made them an instant hit.

40 minifigure variants were released in 1978. Today there are more than 11,000!

Brick History

In 1975, the forerunner of the minifigure debuted in sets. These early figures were made from three pieces (plus a hat). They had no faces, and only the suggestion of arms and legs.

FACT STACK

Out of the LEGO colours available in 1978, yellow was chosen for minifigures as it was considered the best choice to represent all skin tones.

The fundamental minifigure form has not changed since it was perfected in 1978.

The unique design of the LEGO minifigure was first protected by a patent in Denmark in 1977.

FUN 5

Early minifigure tools still in use today

1 Axe (1978)

2 Sword (1978)

3 Shovel (1978)

4 Radio (1979)

5 Spanner (1979)

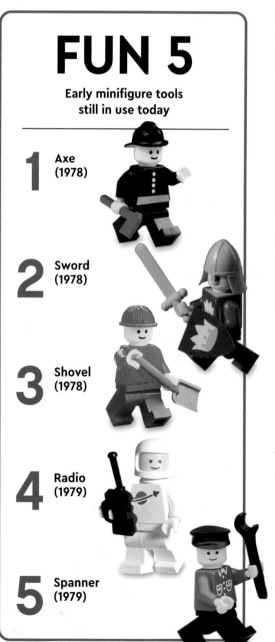

I LIKE YOUR HAIR.

I LIKE *YOUR* HAIR!

REALLY?!

Until 1983, there were only two minifigure haircuts: pigtails and side parting. There have been more than 300 styles since.

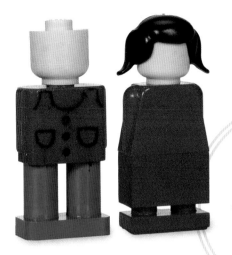

WOW!

A team of LEGO designers, led by Jens Nygård Knudsen, made 50 different minifigure prototypes from plastic and tin before arriving at the final design.

The boxes of several 1979 sets show minifigures wearing a hairpiece that was never released. The final element was more intricately shaped to suggest ears.

Q What are LEGO minifigures made from?

A Just like LEGO bricks, minifigures are made from a tough plastic compound called acrylonitrile butadiene styrene, known as ABS for short.

MAYBE BABIES

As well as appearing as adults in LEGOLAND® sets, some of the first minifigures were cast as infants in larger scale LEGO® Homemaker sets, alongside tall "building figures".

THE MAKING OF A MINIFIGURE

THE DESIGN PROCESS

It can take a whole year to design and make a minifigure! From coming up with new ideas to testing the finished product, every step is vital to make each minifigure the best it can be...

1 GETTING TOGETHER

When a new minifigure is needed, LEGO designers and other team members get together to share ideas. They look at what has worked in the past and try to spot opportunities that no one has thought of before!

2 QUICK ON THE DRAW

As the team discusses the new minifigure's role and story, designers put pen to paper (or stylus to tablet) and start to sketch out rough ideas.

3 A SPLASH OF COLOUR

Once the team has chosen its favourite ideas, a graphic designer will develop them further, adding colour and head-to-toe details.

4 MAKING MODELS

If a design calls for a new hairpiece, accessory, or body part, an element designer will get to work creating the new design as a three-dimensional computer model. This can be used to make test versions using a 3D printer, or moulded prototypes that are very close to the finished product.

5 BIGGER FIGURES

To help get the shape of a new element exactly right, the team will sometimes review extra-large versions, compatible with extra-large minifigures that never leave LEGO HQ!

The classic minifigure form has not changed since 1978, but the details and decorations that make each one special still offer plenty of scope for new ideas.

I'M GLAD MY LUTE SURVIVED THE SAFETY TESTING!

9 COMMENTS WELCOME

As well as assessing the graphics themselves, the team will also invite feedback from other people inside the LEGO Group. Sometimes, they will also share the design with a handful of lucky LEGO fans to get their opinions, too!

8 MAKING IT STICK

The graphic designer finalizes the printed decorations on a standard minifigure template, adding any accessories that also require decoration. This is done digitally, but the designs are also printed as stickers that can be applied to blank minifigures for review.

10 INTO PRODUCTION

When everyone has had their say and all the necessary tweaks have been made, the minifigure is finally ready for production! Quality tests will continue in the factory, to make sure every minifigure is as good as the last.

7 SAFETY ASSURED

When new elements are involved, the team also works closely with the LEGO Group's safety experts. Any new parts have to go through rigorous quality and safety checks that involve heating, crushing, and twisting them to their limits!

6 SECRET STANDARDS

All through the process, the team is constantly reviewing the design and checking it against the big book of minifigure guidelines. These written standards ensure quality and consistency across the LEGO range, and are known only to insiders!

TOP SECRET

MINIFIGURE OR NOT?

Many LEGO themes feature minifigure characters, but not every character in those themes is a minifigure! Characters made from non-standard parts are known as "creature figures" and come in lots of different shapes and sizes.

This **policewoman** is a minifigure because she has all the standard minifigure parts: torso, arms, legs, and a head.

This **skeleton** is classed as a creature figure, not a minifigure, because it does not have a standard torso or any standard limbs.

This **Scurrier** is also classed as a creature figure because it does not have any standard minifigure parts at all!

9,610,000,000

Approximate distance from the Earth to the Moon, measured in minifigures.

Brick History

In 2019, classic Space minifigures made a comeback in THE LEGO® MOVIE 2™, wearing white, yellow and – for the first time – pink!

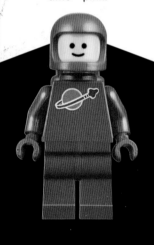

FACT STACK

In 1978, the first LEGO® Space minifigures wore either red or white outfits.

Yellow spacesuits appeared in 1979, then blue and black in 1984.

Black spacesuits are the rarest, appearing in fewer than 10 sets.

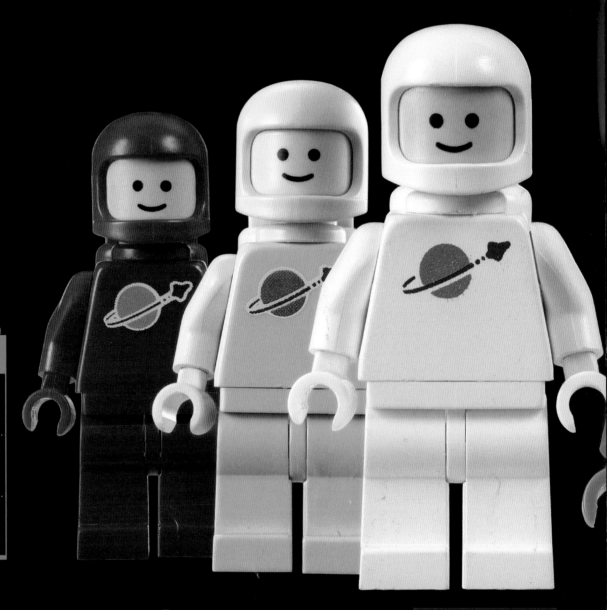

KEY DATES

1987
The LEGO® Futuron space minifigures are the first to get helmets with transparent visors.

1992
The first LEGO Space minifigures to have special face prints appear in Space Police sets.

1993
Ice Planet 2002 sets are the first to distinguish between male and female astronauts.

2011
Space minifigures get double-sided face prints, so they can look alarmed in the Alien Conquest Battle Pack!

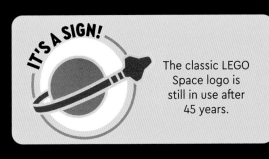

IT'S A SIGN!

The classic LEGO Space logo is still in use after 45 years.

BROKEN BENNY

Benny from the THE LEGO® MOVIE™ was based on the original blue Space minifigure from 1984. His helmet was designed to look like it was broken due to it being played with a great deal, for that authentic toybox vibe!

WOW!

Classic-style space minifigures didn't wear green until 2014's Exo Suit (set 21109), a fan-designed LEGO® Ideas set.

FLYING COLOURS

Red alert! And yellow! And blue! In 1978, these explorers made a giant leap for LEGO® minifigures. Boldly going where no bricks had gone before, they were the first to venture into LEGOLAND Space. They have remained beloved figures for light years since.

MINIFIGURES THROUGH THE AGES

LEGO® Minifigures have taken inspiration from historical (and prehistorical) humans from as early as 10,000 BCE. These characters range from ancient cave people to modern scientists.

Start here!

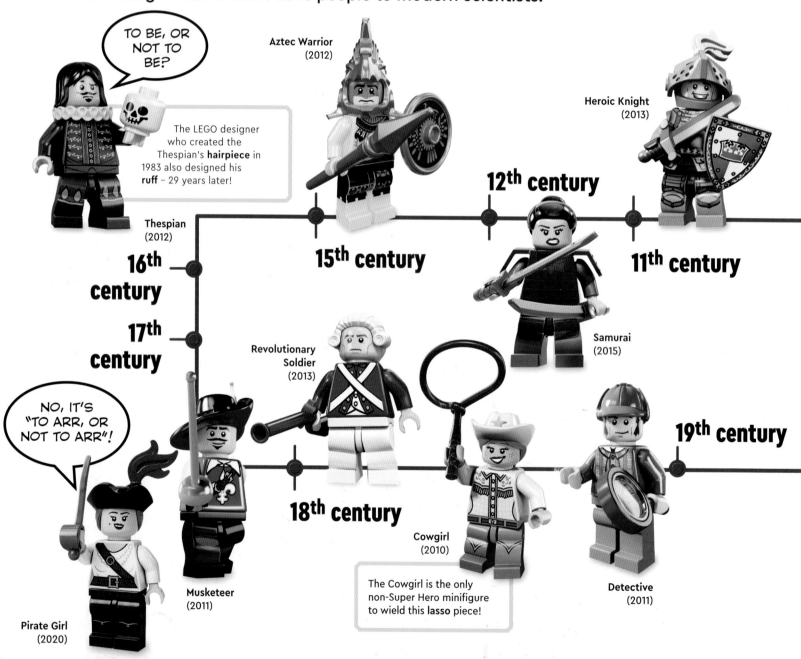

TO BE, OR NOT TO BE?

Aztec Warrior (2012)

The LEGO designer who created the Thespian's **hairpiece** in 1983 also designed his **ruff** – 29 years later!

Heroic Knight (2013)

Thespian (2012)

12th century

16th century

15th century

11th century

17th century

Samurai (2015)

Revolutionary Soldier (2013)

NO, IT'S "TO ARR, OR NOT TO ARR"!

19th century

18th century

Cowgirl (2010)

Detective (2011)

Musketeer (2011)

The Cowgirl is the only non-Super Hero minifigure to wield this **lasso** piece!

Pirate Girl (2020)

UG?

Caveman
(2010)

NO HUGS UNTIL YOU'VE SHAVED.

Cave Woman
(2011)

c.10,000 BCE

Spartan Warrior
(2010)

c.500-400 BCE

Pharaoh
(2010)

The Pharaoh's **snake-topped staff** was designed especially for this regal minifigure.

c.300-100 BCE

Egyptian Queen
(2011)

The Viking Woman's **horns** were intended as a one-off piece, but they have become a versatile element. It is a good job they are detachable, as historians believe Vikings didn't actually have horned helmets!

Viking Woman
(2012)

9th–10th century

5th century

ET TU, BRUTE?

c.50 BCE–4th century

WHO ARE YOU CALLING A BRUTE?

Hun Warrior
(2014)

Roman Emperor
(2013)

Roman Commander
(2013)

Disco Diva
(2015)

20th century

Programmer
(2019)

21st century

I CAN SEE THROUGH TIME!

Hollywood Starlet
(2013)

Hippie
(2012)

The fashion-forward Hippie is the first minifigure ever to don **tie-dye clothes**, an iconic element of 1960s style.

Drone boy
(2020)

153

WE COME IN PIECES!

In the LEGO® Space universe, aliens and robots come in many shapes and sizes. Some are peaceful, but others are preparing for battle!

MEET THE MARTIANS

In 2001, LEGO® Life on Mars sets mixed astronauts with brand-new Martian figures. These friendly aliens featured new parts and colours and were named after real stars and constellations.

MY NAME IS VEGA.

Q	Who was the first alien minifigure?
A	Alpha Draconis and his fellow U.F.O. aliens made first contact in 1996. They wore unique, out-of-this-world helmets, with scary printed faces underneath.

FUN 5

Cosmic citizen collectibles

1. **Space Alien** (Series 3), 2011

2. **Classic Alien** (Series 6), 2012

3. **Alien Trooper** (Series 13), 2015

4. **Alien Villainess** (Series 8), 2011

5. **Space Creature** (Series 22), 2022

Space Alien

Classic Alien

FACT STACK

The first LEGO Space droids were brick-built helpers in 1985 sets.

A 1986 set was called Alien Moon Stalker, but it did not include any aliens.

It was 1996 before LEGO aliens were identified in LEGO Space U.F.O. sets.

REALLY?!

The scary Space Skulls starred in a 2008 LEGO® Factory set, piloting giant, skull-shaped spaceships!

SMALLEST ALIEN

One-eyed Clinger from Alien Conquest sets

Brick History

The first minifigure designed to represent a robot was the Spyrius Droid from 1994. He was also the first minifigure to have printed legs.

245633

The prisoner number of escaped alien crook Jawson, who was on the loose in LEGO® Space Police sets during 2010.

Alien Trooper

Alien Villainess

Space Creature

THE MAGIC OF MINIFIGURES

Every minifigure has a touch of magic, but these fauns, fairies, witches, and wish-granters have a little bit more than most.

FACT STACK

The first minifigure wizards and witches cast their spell in LEGO® Castle sets of the 1990s.

In 1999, LEGO® BELVILLE™ took a magical turn as witches and fairies joined its doll range.

Magnifo (set 41525) is one of three brick-built wizards in the 2014 LEGO® Mixels™ range.

Brick History

In 2012, the LEGO® *The Lord of the Rings*™ and *The Hobbit*™ themes launched, reimagining magical characters such as Gandalf the Grey in minifigure form.

REALLY?!

In the LEGO® NEXO KNIGHTS™ theme, the wizard Merlok turned into a computer program called Merlok 2.0!

MYTHS AND LEG-ENDS

The magical, mystical Faun from the LEGO® Minifigures theme has a special leg piece used in no other set. Though his goat-like limbs are slim, his hooves still fit onto LEGO studs.

Q Are there magical beings in LEGO® NINJAGO®?

A Lots! The scary Skull Sorcerer is a master of dark magic, while Nadakhan is a wish-twisting genie, known as a djinn.

ELF DISCOVERY

LEGO® Elves was the first mini doll theme to feature magical characters. Between 2015 and 2018, it told tales of Elves, dragons, goblins, and flying horses!

Naida the Water Elf

Miku the Baby Dragon

Roblin the Goblin

Golden Glow the Pegasus

GOATEE BEARD? I'VE GOT A GOATY *EVERYTHING!*

FUN 5

Collectible Minifigure spellcasters

1 **Fairy** (Series 8), 2012

2 **Leprechaun** (Series 6), 2012

3 **Wizard** (Series 12), 2014

4 **Genie Girl** (Series 12), 2014

5 **Wacky Witch** (Series 14), 2015

8 different wizards have appeared in LEGO Castle sets since 1995.

WOW!

Amset-Ra is the Pharaoh at the heart of 2011's Pharaoh's Quest theme. His six magical treasures are guarded by enchanted warriors such as Flying Mummies.

MINIFIGURE FIRSTS

These pioneers have all earned their place in history by taking LEGO® minifigures into new areas of innovation, fashion, and play!

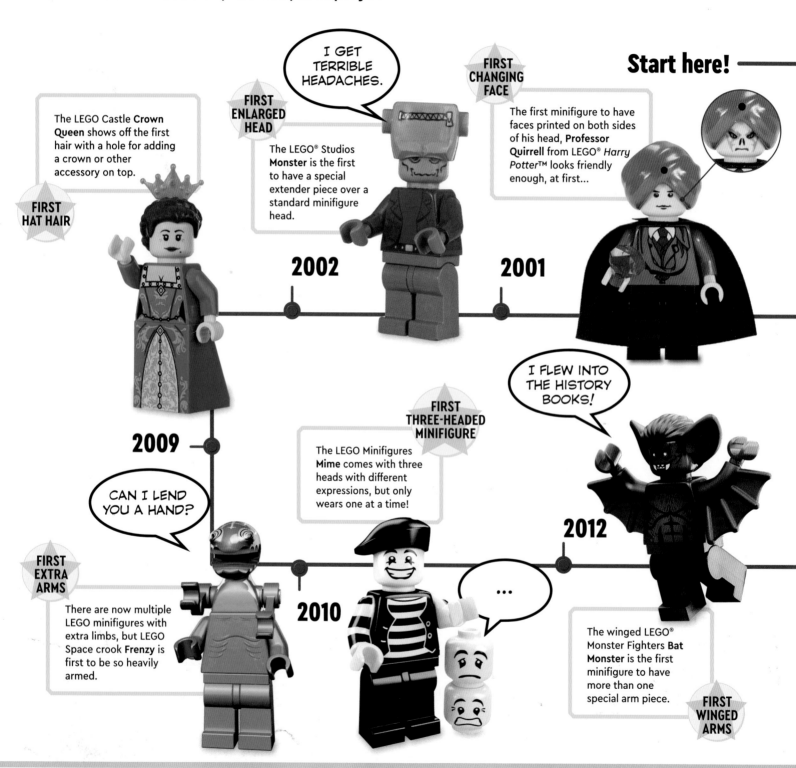

Start here!

I GET TERRIBLE HEADACHES.

FIRST ENLARGED HEAD

The LEGO® Studios **Monster** is the first to have a special extender piece over a standard minifigure head.

FIRST CHANGING FACE

The first minifigure to have faces printed on both sides of his head, **Professor Quirrell** from LEGO® *Harry Potter*™ looks friendly enough, at first...

FIRST HAT HAIR

The LEGO Castle **Crown Queen** shows off the first hair with a hole for adding a crown or other accessory on top.

2002

2001

2009

CAN I LEND YOU A HAND?

FIRST EXTRA ARMS

There are now multiple LEGO minifigures with extra limbs, but LEGO Space crook **Frenzy** is first to be so heavily armed.

FIRST THREE-HEADED MINIFIGURE

The LEGO Minifigures **Mime** comes with three heads with different expressions, but only wears one at a time!

I FLEW INTO THE HISTORY BOOKS!

2010

...

2012

The winged LEGO® Monster Fighters **Bat Monster** is the first minifigure to have more than one special arm piece.

FIRST WINGED ARMS

158

'TIS LUCKY MY SURNAME IS REDBEARD.

FIRST FACIAL HAIR

LEGO® Pirates such as **Captain Redbeard** are the first minifigures to have beards and individual expressions.

1989

MY TAILOR IS VERY CAPE-ABLE!

FIRST FABRIC

The first minifigures to wear fabric capes are the LEGO Castle **Dragon Masters**. Fabric pieces have also been used for ponchos, skirts, and more.

1993

Worn by **Majisto the Wizard**, the first detachable beard piece fits onto the torso at the neck.

FIRST FLOWING BEARD

FIRST FOOTWEAR

LEGO® Aquazone **Aquanauts** are the first to don footwear – flippers! Other minifigures go on to wear ice skates, roller skates, and skis on their feet.

Minifigures start to wear shades in 1993, but this LEGO Town **Shuttle Scientist** is the first to sport ordinary spectacles.

FIRST GLASSES

1995

FIRST GUIDE DOG

This minifigure with a visual impairment is the first to have an assistance **dog** with a special harness.

2021

FIRST 'BLADE' LEG

Modern **prosthetics** arrived in LEGO® City when this shopper stepped in to its first Supermarket set.

2016

FIRST WHEELCHAIR

Brick-built wheelchairs had featured in earlier sets, but the first **wheelchair piece** is used by a minifigure in a LEGO City People Pack (set 60134).

2022

THE WILD BUNCH

These LEGO® characters are no ordinary creatures. In their play themes, animals talk, wear clothes, and have amazing adventures!

Eagles
Other tribes of birds include the Ravens and the Vultures.

FACT STACK

The first LEGO® DUPLO® animal figures were a dog and a cat, found in several 1970s sets.

Unikitty from THE LEGO MOVIE is a rare example of a brick-built animal character.

Two wolf-headed Anubis Warriors appear in 2011's Pharaoh's Quest theme.

27
pieces used to build Spinlyn the Spider from LEGO® Legends of Chima™, making her the biggest minifigure ever!

FANTASTIC BEASTS

For centuries, explorers have searched for mythical animals. If they just checked out the LEGO Minifigures line, they would find a Minotaur, a Yeti, and the unmistakable tracks of a "Square Foot"!

Sabre-toothed Tigers
One of two tribe species extinct in the real world, along with Mammoths.

Phoenixes
The only Legends of Chima tribe to be based on a mythical creature.

FUN 5
Collectible critter costumes

1 Lizard Man (Series 5), 2011

2 Bunny Suit Guy (Series 7), 2012

3 Bumblebee Girl (Series 10), 2013

DON'T BE ALARMED, BE A LLAMA!

4 Shark Suit Guy (Series 15), 2016

5 Llama Costume Girl (Series 20), 2020

THE TRIBES OF CHIMA

Animals from 21 tribes appeared in LEGO Chima sets between 2013 and 2015, including...

Lions
One of 14 mammal tribes, alongside Wolves, Beavers, Bears, and Bats.

Crocodiles
The only other cold-blooded tribes are the Scorpions and Spiders.

AWESOME!

The animal-packed LEGO® Monkie Kid™ theme includes monkey, pig, bull, and spider characters – plus a robotic rabbit (pictured)!

LOOK CLOSER

Most LEGO Legends of Chima animal heads fit over a standard minifigure head with two printed faces. This allows different expressions to show through the eyeholes.

Piece particulars

In 2011, new head and tail parts were created for Serpentine characters in the LEGO NINJAGO theme. The snaking tails have since been used in the LEGO NEXO KNIGHTS range and LEGO Minifigures series.

FAB FRIENDS

The animal characters of LEGO® Fabuland were the first LEGO figures to have individual names and stories. Between 1979 and 1989, more than 40 characters appeared in almost 100 sets, including...

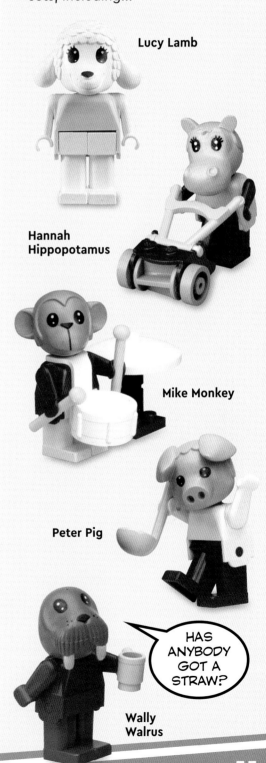

Lucy Lamb

Hannah Hippopotamus

Mike Monkey

Peter Pig

HAS ANYBODY GOT A STRAW?

Wally Walrus

Sea creatures

1   **LEGO shark (*Squalus legodtus*).**
    Grey sharks were widespread in the
    era of LEGO Pirates and can still be
    seen in LEGO City harbour. White sharks
    have also been spotted off LEGO Town.

2   **LEGO fish (*Piscis legodtus*)**. The most common
    variety of LEGO fish is silver-scaled, and ranges as far
    as the LEGO® *Star Wars*™ universe.
    Look out for orange and green species, too.

3   **LEGO octopus (*Octopus legodtus*).**
    Black and red varieties of LEGO octopus have been
    spotted by LEGO Pirates and others, but only the
    LEGO® Agents have identified a glow-in-the-dark
    one!

4   **LEGO crab (*Carcinus legodtus*).** Red crabs are
    local to LEGO® BELVILLE™, but light orange
    examples range across LEGO City, Heartlake City,
    Ninjago Island, and elsewhere.

5   **LEGO crocodile (Crocodylus legodtus).** First
    discovered by LEGO Pirates, snapping crocodiles
    with swishing tails have also been spotted in the
    swamps and jungles that border LEGO City.

Mammals

6   **LEGO horse (*Equus legodtus*).** The
    horse is one of the most widespread
    LEGO species. Since 2012, a more
    athletic breed – given to rearing –
    has become the dominant variety.

7   **LEGO dog (*Canis legodtus*).** Huskies,
    Chihuahuas, Dalmatians, and terriers
    are just some of the LEGO dog breeds
    to be seen in LEGO City or further
    afield with LEGO minifigure owners.

8   **LEGO cat (*Felis legodta*).** LEGO cats
    are most popular as pets in LEGO
    BELVILLE, but can also be seen alongside
    LEGO witches and being rescued
    from trees by LEGO City firefighters.

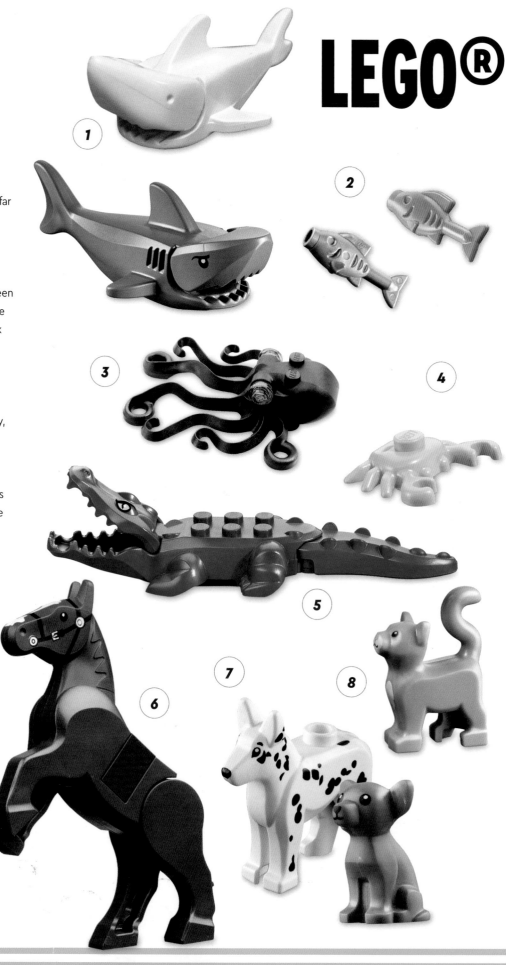

LEGO®

ANIMALS

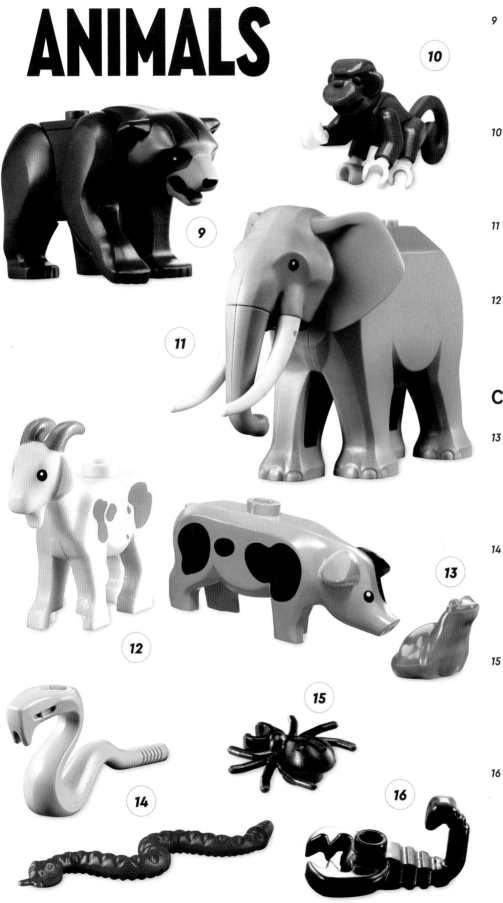

9   **LEGO bear** *(Ursus legodtus).* LEGO Town Arctic explorers were the first to encounter polar bears, while the LEGO City Forest Police have regular run-ins with mighty brown bears.

10   **LEGO monkeys (Simius legodtus).** Large, curly-tailed monkeys dot the coasts charted by LEGO Pirates, while a smaller species now swings from the trees around LEGO City.

11   **LEGO elephant** *(Elefantus legodtus).* Only the LEGO Adventurers and the LEGO City Wildlife Rescue team have encountered LEGO elephants.

12   **LEGO farm animals** *(Domesticus legodtus).* LEGO goats, pigs, and cows were all reared in the LEGO Castle era, with pigs, cows, and sheep now a familiar sight in more rural parts of LEGO City.

Creepy crawlies

13   **LEGO frog** *(Rana legodta).* Frogs abound in a variety of LEGO environments, from the era of LEGO Castle to modern Heartlake City. They have even made the giant leap into LEGO Space!

14   **LEGO snake** *(Serpens legodtus).* The common LEGO snake spans many habitats and is most often coloured red. Its fanged cousin comes in many colours and is largely restricted to Ninjago Island.

15   **LEGO spider** *(Aranea legodta).* More than 10 different colours of spider have been seen across a range of LEGO habitats, including glow-in-the-dark specimens found by LEGO Monster Fighters.

16   **LEGO scorpion** *(Scorpio legodtus).* Most often encountered by LEGO Adventurers, scorpions are also found on Ninjago Island. Rare, brightly coloured varieties have been recorded further afield.

FASHION STATEMENTS

LEGO® characters always dress to impress in a range of outfits, from the stylish to the outlandish. Here are some of their best and boldest fashion choices.

Brick History

In 1978, the first minifigures all wore hats, helmets, or hair in pigtails. The classic short-back-and-sides hairpiece came into fashion the next year.

3,581

The number of sets that black trousers have been found in since they first appeared in 1978, making them the most popular trousers for minifigures.

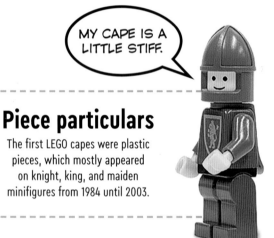

MY CAPE IS A LITTLE STIFF.

Piece particulars

The first LEGO capes were plastic pieces, which mostly appeared on knight, king, and maiden minifigures from 1984 until 2003.

LOOK CLOSER

Some minifigures wear clothes that hark back to earlier LEGO eras. This funky top showing a classic LEGO astronaut appears in 24 sets.

AWESOME!

"Where Are My Pants?" Guy from THE LEGO MOVIE Minifigures range is more famous for the clothes he doesn't wear than the ones he does!

FUN 5
LEGO Minifigures in traditional costumes

1 Bagpiper
(Series 7), 2012

2 Flamenco Dancer
(Series 6), 2012)

3 Hula Dancer
(Series 3), 2011

4 Lederhosen Guy
(Series 8), 2012

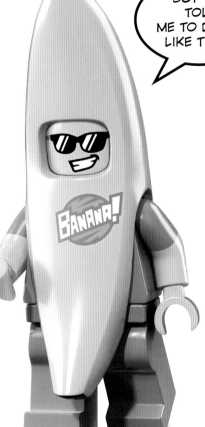

BUT YOU TOLD ME TO DRESS LIKE THIS...

MOST FASHIONABLE MINIFIGURE

Trendsetter

NO, I SAID WEAR SOMETHING APPEALING.

WOW!

Lots of LEGO Minifigures like to dress as their favourite food! They include Peapod Girl, Watermelon Dude, and Banana Guy.

FACT STACK

2011's Punk Rocker Minifigure had safety pins in his jeans and a pink Mohican haircut!

More than 30 minifigures have dressed as Santa – including Darth Vader!

Emma is the fashionista among the LEGO® Friends, and runs her own boutique.

5 **Kimono Girl**
(Series 4), 2011

KEY HATS

1975
An early style in minifigure millinery, the **Stetson**, or cowboy hat, can still be found in present-day sets.

1980
A chef is one of the first minifigures to wear a **top hat**! Most LEGO cooks since 1980 have opted for the more traditional chef's hat.

1989
Shiver me timbers! **Pirate hats** with and without skull and crossbones appear.

1995
This LEGO Castle King is the first minifigure to wear a piece in **glitzy chrome gold**.

2015
Construction workers are the first City-dwellers to wear **hats with built-in hairstyles!**

A GALAXY OF STARS

From Luke and Leia to The Mandalorian and more, the heroes of the *Star Wars* saga are some of the world's most iconic characters. They are all instantly recognizable as LEGO® minifigures, too.

I'VE GOT A GOOD FEELING ABOUT YOU, KID!

50

Approximate age difference in years between Young and Old Han Solo.

ROYAL EXCLUSIVE

Padmé Amidala wears her full Queen of Naboo regalia in Gungan Sub (set 9499). Her circular skirt has never been used in any other set.

LOOK CLOSER

The 2014 variant of C-3PO includes the restraining bolt placed on him by Jawas to keep him under control!

FACT STACK

There are now more than 1,300 different LEGO *Star Wars* minifigures!

All new parts were needed to create the R2-D2 figure in 1999.

Jar Jar Binks was the first minifigure to have a specially shaped head mould.

AWESOME!

Five classic minifigures were reissued to mark 20 years of LEGO *Star Wars* in 2019, each coming with a special display stand.

FUN 5

Strange species of the LEGO *Star Wars* world with specially crafted heads

1 Mon Calamari (Admiral Ackbar)

2 Ithorian (Jedi Master)

3 Kaminoan (Taun We)

4 Ewok (Wicket)

5 Um... (Maz Kanata)

Brick History

From 1999 to 2004, most LEGO *Star Wars* minifigures had yellow hands and faces. The first to have a realistic skin tone was Lando Calrissian in 2003.

REALLY?!

In Jabba's Sail Barge (set 75020) R2-D2 is built with an extra piece to turn him into a serving tray!

Q | What is the rarest LEGO minifigure?

A | That is probably the solid silver C-3PO made to celebrate the 30th anniversary of *Star Wars* in 2007. Only one was ever made, along with five in solid gold.

THIS WOULD GO GREAT WITH A WOOKIEE COOKIE!

WOW!

There are more than 50 minifigure versions and variants of Luke Skywalker, including one enjoying a refreshing drink of blue milk!

KEY DATES

1999
The first LEGO *Star Wars* sets include Qui-Gon Jinn, Luke Skywalker, Padmé Amidala, and other minifigure heroes.

2008
Sets based on animated TV series *Star Wars: The Clone Wars* follow the adventures of Obi-Wan Kenobi, Anakin Skywalker, and Ahsoka Tano.

2014
A new animated series, *Star Wars Rebels*, spawns LEGO *Star Wars* sets featuring young Ezra Bridger and the crew of the *Ghost*.

2015
Finn and Rey meet old friends Han, Chewie, and Leia as the first LEGO *Star Wars: The Force Awakens* sets are released.

2020
The Mandalorian and his cute green companion, Grogu, are among the first figures to be based on live-action *Star Wars* TV shows.

A HIVE OF FUN AND VILLAINY

Sometimes it's fun to play the bad guy... These minifigure meanies make the LEGO® *Star Wars*™ universe a more exciting place to visit!

Brick History

Since 2011, special sets have been given away to mark *Star Wars* Day on 4 May. The star of 2014's set was the video game villain Darth Revan.

FACT STACK

The first LEGO Sith Lord was Darth Maul back in 1999.

Stormtroopers didn't show up in any sets until 2001.

The largest LEGO *Star Wars* villain is Jabba the Hutt.

ROGER, ROGER, ROGER, ROGER, ROGER, ROGER, ROGER...

174

B1 battle droids found in more than 50 different LEGO *Star Wars* sets.

Brick statistics

10,000 limited-edition white Boba Fetts
based on *Star Wars* concept art and given away in 2010

8 Boba variants with printed faces
hidden beneath printed visors

5 Boba variants with plain black heads
visible through helmets with cutaway visors

2 young Bobas
as seen in *Episode II: Attack of the Clones*

1 solid bronze Boba
awarded to a US competition winner in 2010

▌ AWESOME!

Brick-built baddies in the LEGO *Star Wars* universe include spider droids, destroyer droids, and flying imperial probe droids!

Q Which LEGO *Star Wars* set has the most minifigures?

A With 14 Imperials and nine rebels (plus two astromech droids), the 2016 Death Star (set 75159) has more minifigures than any other!

I FEEL YOUR PRESENTS.

MOST FESTIVE SITH LORD

Santa Darth Vader (set 75056)

WOW!

The General Grievous figure is made from eight special pieces, none of which is used to make any other character.

REALLY?!

Sith Lord Darth Sidious (a.k.a. the Emperor) appears in 17 sets, but smiles in only one of them!

FUN 5

Stylish super troopers

1 Captain Phasma (2015)

2 Mimban Stormtrooper (2018)

3 Shadow Trooper (2019)

4 Sith Jet Trooper (2020)

5 Artillery Stormtrooper (2021)

Chef (1979)

OOOPS, I DROPPED A BEET.

Fortune Teller (2013)

Janitor (2016)

TV News Reporter (2011)

Admiral (1992)

Rapper (2011)

HEY! THAT'S MY JOB.

ALL WALKS OF LIFE

Air Traffic Controller (1988)

Painter (2011)

Horserider (1986)

King (2004)

Librarian (2013)

Waiter (1990)

Ice Cream Seller (2022)

Firefighter (2015)

Crook (2013)

Athlete (2022)

Judge (2013)

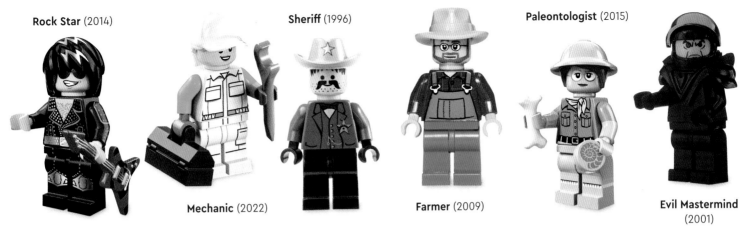

Rock Star (2014)

Sheriff (1996)

Paleontologist (2015)

Mechanic (2022)

Farmer (2009)

Evil Mastermind
(2001)

They may be small, but no job is too big for these LEGO® minifigures. From kings to crooks, they've got every vacancy filled!

Demolition Worker (2015)

Veterinarian
(2021)

Scientist (1999)

Ninja (2010)

Jester (2008)

Wrestler (2010)

Stunt Pilot (1993)

WHY WALK
WHEN YOU
CAN DANCE?

Football Referee (1998)

Astronaut
(2022)

Clown (2010)

Carpenter (2015)

Barber (2015)

Diver (2020)

LEGO Store
Worker (2020)

Ballerina (2016)

WE ARE NINJA

In 2021, the LEGO® NINJAGO® theme celebrated 10 years of brave warriors doing battle with snakes, spirits, Sky Pirates, and more!

WOW!

When the ninja had their first undersea adventure, Nya transformed into a mighty water spirit!

DON'T LOOK NOW, BUT THE OTHER PAGE IS FULL OF TERRIBLE VILLAINS.

1,210
megawatts generated by Jay when he uses his full electrical power.

DON'T LOOK NOW, BUT THE OTHER PAGE IS FULL OF TERRIBLE VILLAINS.

Zane   **Jay**   **Lloyd**

Master Wu

REALLY?!

Before he was a ninja, Lloyd wanted to be a villain. It seemed the obvious choice for the son of evil Lord Garmadon!

Brick History

In 2021, special gold-coloured versions of all six ninja and Master Wu could be found in a series of tenth anniversary sets.

Cole   **Kai**   **Nya**

AWESOME!

Over the years, wise Master Wu has been turned into evil Techno Wu, moody Teen Wu, and supercute Baby Wu!

FUN 5

Careers of Ninjago villains before they turned bad

1 Lord Garmadon: peaceful teacher.

2 OverBorg: brilliant inventor.

3 Master Chen: noodle-bar owner.

4 Harumi: quiet princess.

5 Nadakhan: pirate (OK, still bad).

Brick History

The Overlord is the oldest villain in the Ninjago world. He was created at the same time as the island itself, and then banished beneath the sea.

BIGGEST BADDIE

Crystal King (set 71772)

Lord Garmadon

Nadakhan

Overborg

Master Chen

Harumi

Q Why did Pythor change colour?

A Pythor used to be purple, but he was bleached white by the stomach acid of a monster that swallowed him. Ugh!

LOOK CLOSER

As if he wasn't scary enough, the Skull Sorceror's cloak spells out 'DEAD RISE' in the Ninjargon language!

FANTASTIC FIGURES AND WHERE TO FIND THEM

More than 350 magical minifigures have enlarged the LEGO® Harry Potter™ theme since 2001 – alongside all sorts of special figures depicting giants, creatures, chess pieces, and more!

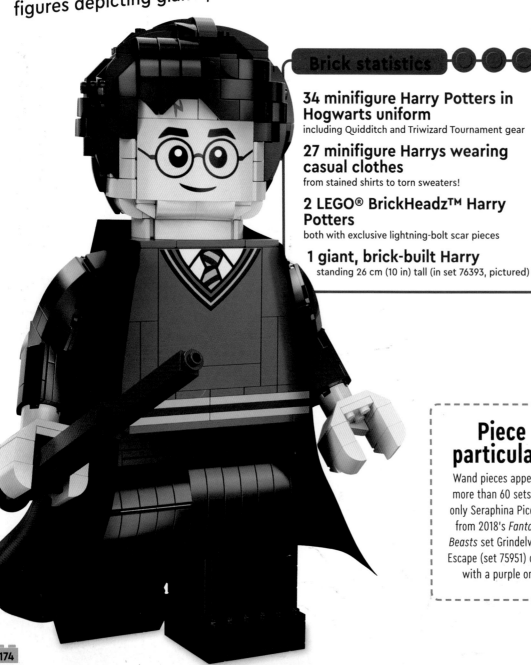

Brick statistics ● ● ●

34 minifigure Harry Potters in Hogwarts uniform
including Quidditch and Triwizard Tournament gear

27 minifigure Harrys wearing casual clothes
from stained shirts to torn sweaters!

2 LEGO® BrickHeadz™ Harry Potters
both with exclusive lightning-bolt scar pieces

1 giant, brick-built Harry
standing 26 cm (10 in) tall (in set 76393, pictured)

FACT STACK

From 2001 to 2003, most LEGO Harry Potter minifigures had yellow hands and faces.

Two waves of collectible LEGO Minifigures featured Harry Potter characters in 2018 and 2020.

In 2021, golden minifigures were included in seven sets to mark 20 years since the first LEGO Harry Potter sets and the first Harry Potter movie.

Piece particulars

Wand pieces appear in more than 60 sets, but only Seraphina Picquery from 2018's *Fantastic Beasts* set Grindelwald's Escape (set 75951) comes with a purple one!

NEW HEIGHTS

Harry and his chums have been depicted with three different lengths of minifigure legs over the years. Medium-length legs were introduced for the characters in the collectible Minifigures series in 2018, and reached other sets not long after.

24

unique microfigures in 2018's enormous Hogwarts Castle (set 71043). Lord Voldemort has never looked so harmless!

REALLY?!

Harry, Hermione, and Ron do battle with a full set of brick-built chess pieces in 2021's Hogwarts Wizard's Chess (set 76392)!

WOW!

There have been six different Hagrid figures since 2001, each one standing a whole head taller than most minifigures!

LOOK CLOSER

Newt Scamander's collectible Minifigure is printed with a fantastic beast called a Bowtruckle crawling out of his overcoat!

In 2020, Forbidden Forest: Umbridge's Encounter (set 75967) not only introduced new Centaur figures, but also a brick-built version of Hagrid's giant half-brother, Grawp!

AWESOME!

Prehistoric LEGO® beasts

1   **LEGO DUPLO dinosaurs.** The first
LEGO dinosaurs lived in LEGO DUPLO
sets from the late 1990s. More
preschool than prehistoric, these
creatures had more chance of getting
chewed themselves than of biting
anyone else!

2   **Dino Island.** In 2000, the LEGO®
Adventurers took a trip to
Dino Island, where Johnny Thunder
and his fellow explorers discovered
the blocky footprints of tyrannosaurs,
triceratopses, and stegosauruses.

3   **Adaptable dinos.** In 2001, a dedicated
LEGO® Dinosaurs theme featured
four-in-one dino models such as the
aquatic lizard Mosasaurus (set 6721),
which could be rebuilt as an
iguanodon, a postosuchus, and
a dimetrodon.

FOR DINOS

4 **Double trouble.** The Dino Attack and Dino 2010 themes were launched in 2005, in the US and Europe respectively. The sets had some differences, but shared the same rampaging raptors and a T-rex with light-up eyes.

5 **LEGO® Dino.** In 2012, the daring Dino Defence team battled prehistoric beasts in the LEGO Dino theme. Their quarry included new designs for flying pteranodons, plus a new coelophysis dino with stripes.

6 **THE LEGO MOVIE 2.**
Raptors from the LEGO Dino theme got a bold, blue makeover in 2019, when they went into space on board Rex's Rexplorer (set 70835)!

CREATURE FEATURE

Some LEGO® animals come fully formed, but these brick beasts are all built to be wild!

Brick History

In 2014, the LEGO Group gave employees a gift set of brick birds native to the UK, China, the USA, Singapore, and Denmark, to celebrate having offices in all those countries.

FACT STACK

One of the first LEGO brick-built animals came in Cowboy & Pony (set 806) in 1964.

The first LEGO Castle knights rode brick-built horses in two 1970s sets.

Fearsome Legend Beasts were among the brick-built creatures in LEGO Legends of Chima.

2

Number of pieces needed to make a LEGO fly – like the one on the tongue of this LEGO Creator Chameleon (set 30477) from 2017!

WOW!

LEGO® Creator 3in1 sets such as 2022's Majestic Tiger (set 31129) can be made into three different animals – in this case a tiger, a red panda, and a koi carp!

FUN 5
LEGO NINJAGO dragons

1 The **Fusion Dragon** has the powers of both its riders – Fire ninja Kai and Water ninja Nya.

2 The ghostly **Morro Dragon** was the first NINJAGO dragon to have fabric wings.

3 The **Skull Sorcerer's Dragon** is an enormous flying skeleton with a belly full of spiders!

4 The **Green NRG Dragon** soars through the sky with a wingspan of 57 cm (22 in).

THE ONLY LEGO® TECHNIC ANIMAL

Control Centre II Dinosaur (set 8485)

Piece particulars

Deep Sea Predators (set 4506) from 2004 used rare glow-in-the-dark pieces to make fearsome fish teeth and scary squid bits!

REALLY?!

Far from prehistoric, the 2008 LEGO Creator Stegosaurus (set 4998) contains a light-up brick to create glowing eyes.

PET PROJECT

Some brick-built animals are less wild than others! The LEGO BrickHeadz Pets subtheme includes cats, budgies, goldfish, hamsters, and various breeds of dog.

In 2010 and 2011, LEGO® Atlantis sets pitted minifigure divers against brick-built sea creatures, including an angry angler fish!

AWESOME!

5 The mighty four-headed **Ultra Dragon** is four Elemental Dragons combined into one force!

CHARACTER BUILDING

LEGO® figures don't have to be mini! From purely brick-built characters to articulated action figures, there are many ways to build a big personality.

HO! HO! HO!

FACT STACK

The first brick-built characters could not be posed and had no jointed or moving parts.

Today's buildable characters use parts other than bricks to allow for realistic movement.

There have been more buildable models of Santa Claus than any other character!

Piece particulars

LEGO ball-and-socket joints were introduced in 1970 for connections such as vehicle tow bars. Most buildable figures are made with newer ball-and-socket friction joints, which connect more tightly for poseability.

REALLY?!

Looking good enough to eat, Birthday Buddy (set 40226) is a brick-built cupcake character released in 2016.

FUN 5

Cool parts used in the LEGO Mixels theme (2014–2016)

1 **Volectro** has hair made out of a bush.

2 **Slumbo** has minifigure helmets for eyelids.

3 **Turg** has a tail piece for a tongue.

4 **Forx** has banana pieces for eyebrows.

5 **Dribbal** has a crystal piece as his... Ugh!

Q What is the Character and Creature Building System (CCBS)?

A CCBS is the name for a figure-building system that was introduced by the LEGO Group in 2011. It features jointed "skeleton" parts and snap-on "shell" pieces that can create large, articulated characters and creatures.

KEY DATES

1999
The LEGO Technic Slizer subtheme (also known as Throwbots) introduces buildable figures articulated using large ball-and-socket friction connectors.

2001
The first BIONICLE® buildable figures blend LEGO Technic articulation with unique, characterful mask pieces and a detailed storyline.

2011
LEGO® Hero Factory introduces a new buildable figure system, still based on ball-and-socket joints, but easier to build and stronger in play.

2015
After a four-year break, LEGO® BIONICLE® returns to stores with sturdy new figures based on the LEGO Hero Factory building system.

WOW!
Since 2016, the LEGO BrickHeadz theme has turned everyone from Superman, Santa and even pop stars the Spice Girls into stylized brick-built figures!

13 points of articulation on lava monster Burnzie from LEGO NEXO KNIGHTS Axl's Tower Carrier (set 70322) from 2016.

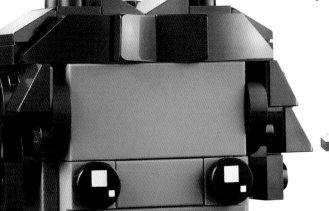

FRESH FACES
In 1974, the first LEGO figures with printed faces and articulated arms were released. Now known as "maxifigures" by fans, they had torsos and legs built from standard bricks, and appeared in more than 30 sets.

ODDEST BRICK-BUILT CHARACTERS
1965's Clowns (set 321)

GO SPORTS!

In a world where croissants are the size of your arm, LEGO® minifigures need to stay in shape. Luckily for them, there's a healthy array of sports-themed sets.

I BETTER GET THIS SHOT NOW THAT EVERYONE IS WATCHING.

REALLY?!

The LEGO Minifigures theme has featured three different cheerleaders, with the latest being a Zombie Cheerleader.

I CHEER WHEN THERE'S A GHOUL!

Brick History

In 2016, the German football team were turned into a LEGO Minifigures series. Fifteen players came with footballs, while manager Joachim Löw came with a unique tactics board.

3

Manchester United soccer legends depicted in The United Trinity (set 6322501) from 2020.

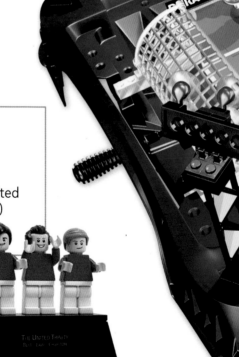

AWESOME!

In 2003, LEGO Sports Gravity Games featured daredevil skateboarder and snowboarder minifigures who could be sent speeding down special ramp pieces.

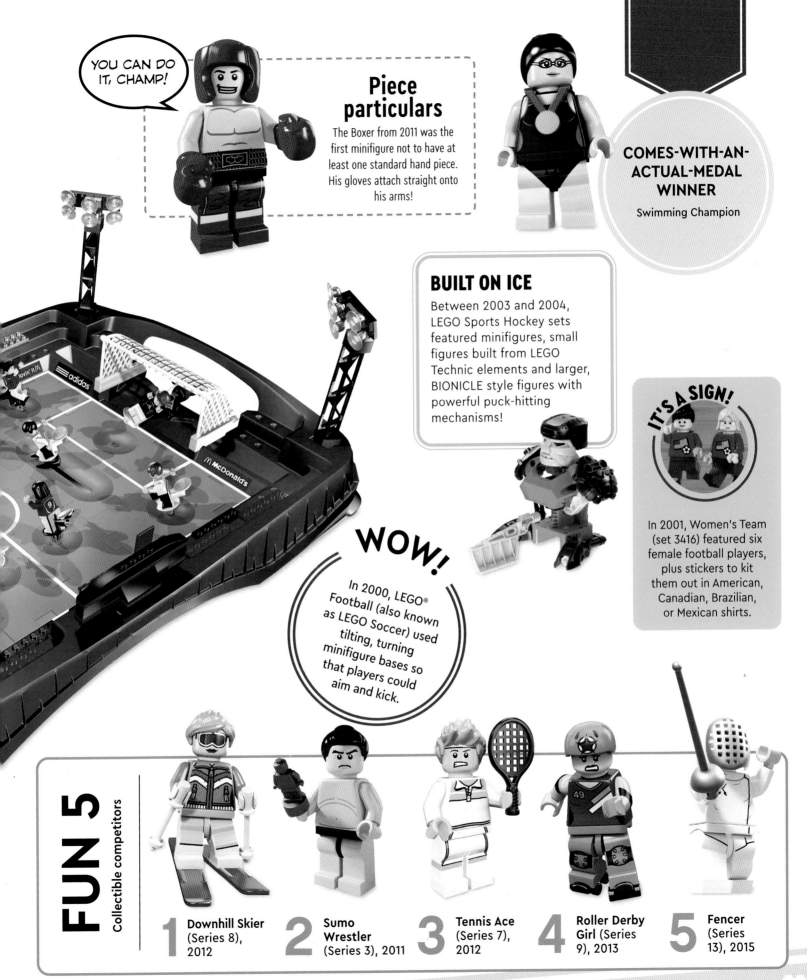

YOU CAN DO IT, CHAMP!

Piece particulars

The Boxer from 2011 was the first minifigure not to have at least one standard hand piece. His gloves attach straight onto his arms!

COMES-WITH-AN-ACTUAL-MEDAL WINNER

Swimming Champion

BUILT ON ICE

Between 2003 and 2004, LEGO Sports Hockey sets featured minifigures, small figures built from LEGO Technic elements and larger, BIONICLE style figures with powerful puck-hitting mechanisms!

IT'S A SIGN!

In 2001, Women's Team (set 3416) featured six female football players, plus stickers to kit them out in American, Canadian, Brazilian, or Mexican shirts.

WOW!

In 2000, LEGO® Football (also known as LEGO Soccer) used tilting, turning minifigure bases so that players could aim and kick.

FUN 5

Collectible competitors

1 Downhill Skier (Series 8), 2012

2 Sumo Wrestler (Series 3), 2011

3 Tennis Ace (Series 7), 2012

4 Roller Derby Girl (Series 9), 2013

5 Fencer (Series 13), 2015

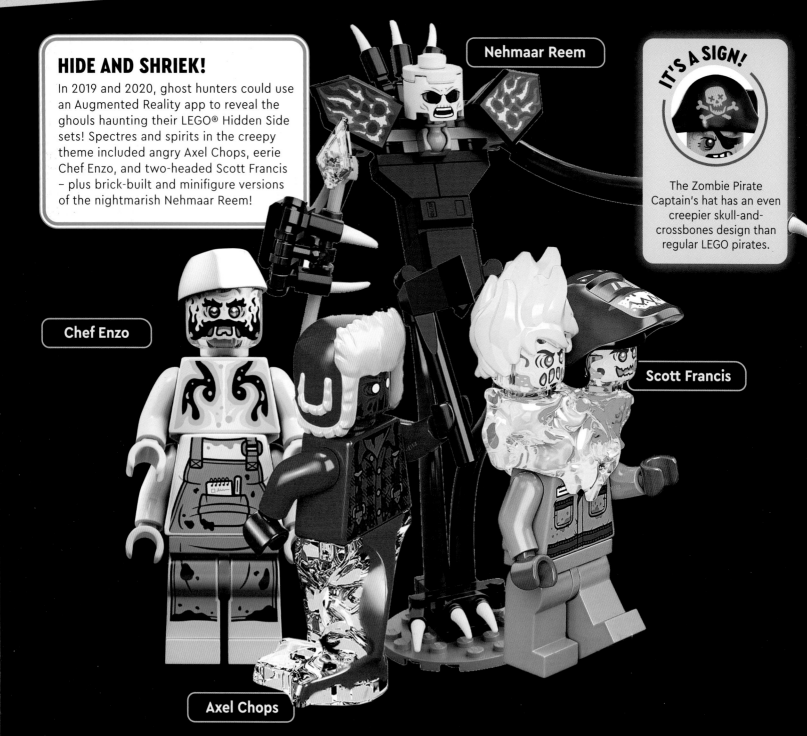

HIDE AND SHRIEK!

In 2019 and 2020, ghost hunters could use an Augmented Reality app to reveal the ghouls haunting their LEGO® Hidden Side sets! Spectres and spirits in the creepy theme included angry Axel Chops, eerie Chef Enzo, and two-headed Scott Francis – plus brick-built and minifigure versions of the nightmarish Nehmaar Reem!

Nehmaar Reem

IT'S A SIGN!

The Zombie Pirate Captain's hat has an even creepier skull-and-crossbones design than regular LEGO pirates.

Chef Enzo

Scott Francis

Axel Chops

FUN 5

Most spine-chilling collectible Minifigures

 1 **Banshee** (Series 14), 2015

 2 **Fright Knight** (Series 19), 2019

 3 **Spectre** (Series 14), 2015

 4 **Medusa** (Series 10), 2013

 5 **Fly Monster** (Series 14), 2015

FACT STACK

LEGO vampires first appeared in LEGO Studios sets in 2002.

The first mummy minifigure haunted the LEGO Adventurers in 1998.

The curse of the LEGO zombies began with one collectible Minifigure in 2010!

Number of sets released in the LEGO® Monster Fighters theme in 2012, complete with six ghosts, a skeleton horse, a swamp creature, and a zombie chef!

Q What do LEGO monsters do in their spare time?

A They chill! The Monster Butler in 2012's Haunted House (set 10228) likes to dance to music. His mummy friends got him into rapping.

LOOK CLOSER

2015's Wolf Guy collectible Minifigure wears the same clothes as 2011's Lumberjack. Could they be the same minifigure, transformed by the moon?

REALLY?!

White head pieces with scary skull designs appear in more than 150 sets – and not always with bodies to rest on!

BOO!

In 1990, the ghost shroud was the first glow-in-the-dark LEGO element. Glowing ghosts have since appeared in 16 scary sets.

HIGH SPIRITS

These creepy characters are happiest raising other minifigures' hairpieces! But don't be scared – they just want to play. For ever and ever and ever and ever...

FACTION PACKED

Since 1978, more than 20 different factions have battled for supremacy in the LEGO® Castle theme, from King's Knights to outlaws and even trolls!

I WENT GREEN BEFORE IT WAS FASHIONABLE!

FACT STACK

There have been more than 400 minifigure variants in the LEGO Castle theme.

In 1987, the Forestmen were the first minifigures to have green legs and torsos.

The first LEGO Castle figure with a name was Majisto the Wizard, conjured up in 1993.

HAIR TO THE THRONE

For the first 20 years of LEGO Castle, only four minifigures had hairpieces instead of helmets. The first were nobles in Knight's Joust (set 383) from 1979.

14 knights in 1978's Castle (set 375) – the most minifigures in any 20th-century set.

SHIELDS UP!

LEGO Castle knights have fought with more than 40 different shields since 1978. Here are just a few from over the years.

Crusaders (1984)

Black Falcons (1984)

Forestmen (1988)

Dragon Knights (1993)

Royal Knights (1995)

Lion Knights (2000)

Shadow Knights (2005)

AWESOME!

In 2004, LEGO® KNIGHTS' KINGDOM™ characters could be collected in minifigure form or as big, buildable action figures.

FUN 5
LEGO Castle fantasy figures

1 Ghost, in sets from 1990.

2 Skeleton, in sets from 1995.

3 Dwarf, in sets from 2007.

4 Troll, in sets from 2008.

5 Giant Troll, in sets from 2008.

FOR ONE KNIGHT ONLY!

WOW!

A 2016 LEGO.com exclusive (set 5004419) featured a **1980s-style knight** and a LEGO Castle timeline in a **special presentation box.**

MOST BLING KING

Crown King (set 7078)

IT'S A SIGN!

The first LEGO Castle knights from 1978 came with a sheet of stickers to decorate their plain grey tabard and shield pieces.

Brick History

In 1993, the Dragon Masters became the first minifigures in any theme to have mismatched arms and legs – a style later taken up by LEGO Castle jesters.

I'M A GOOD GUY, REALLY!

Skeleton Warriors (2007)

Troll Warriors (2007)

King's Knights (2013)

Q Who are the bad guys in early LEGO Castle sets?

A That's entirely up to you! It was not until the 1990s that villainous factions such as the Wolfpack appeared in LEGO Castle sets.

SMALL BUT MIGHTY

Heroes come in all shapes and sizes, but in the world of LEGO® DC Super Heroes, they are all approximately four bricks high!

Q | What is LEGO Robin's true identity?

A | There have been several LEGO Robins, including Tim Drake (also known as "Red Robin"), Dick Grayson, and Damian Wayne. But keep that under your cape!

I'M ROBIN!

NO, I'M ROBIN!

Tim Drake

Dick Grayson

Damian Wayne

REALLY?!
There are more than 10 Superman minifigures, but only one Clark Kent – who is busy changing into Superman!

Brick History

Though the first LEGO DC Super Heroes sets were not released until 2012, exclusive Batman, Superman, and Green Lantern minifigures were given away at special events in 2011.

FACT STACK

There are more than 250 LEGO DC Super Heroes minifigures.

Over half of the minifigures in the theme fight on the side of truth and justice.

Famous Super Heroes depicted in them include Aquaman, the Flash, and several Green Lanterns.

LITTLE WONDER
There have been four different Wonder Woman minifigures, but only 2017 Mighty Micros version comes with short legs, in keeping with the scaled-down style of that theme.

AWESOME!

In 2017, mini dolls of Supergirl, Batgirl, Wonder Woman, and others starred in the DC Super Hero Girls theme!

12 minifigure-scale sets
in the LEGO Batman theme that preceded LEGO DC Super Heroes

11 Batman minifigures
based on live-action movies, including 2022's The Batman (pictured)

10 different masks
worn by Batman in the DC Super Heroes theme, including one with a built-in cape

9 other LEGO themes
in which Batman features, including LEGO DUPLO and THE LEGO MOVIE.

IS IT JUST ME, OR IS IT COLD IN HERE?

WOW!

Pets can be Super Heroes, too! Superman's dog, Krypto, and Ace the Bat-Hound, both appeared in 2018 sets!

FUN 5 Lesser-known heroes

1 Plastic Man (set 5004081)

2 Beast Boy (set 76035)

3 Hawkman (set 76028)

4 Blue Beetle (set 76054)

5 Katana (set 76055)

LOOK CLOSER

Part of an exclusive 2015 gift cube (set 5004077), the rare Lightning Lad minifigure has lightning-bolt eyebrows!

IT'S A SIGN!

Superman's "S-Shield" is actually a Kryptonian family crest. It is also worn by his father, Jor-El, and his cousin, Kara, also known as Supergirl.

BUILT TO BE BADDIES

Super Heroes are nothing without their enemies. This Rogues Gallery causes chaos for the good guys in LEGO® DC Super Heroes sets.

WHAT A BUNCH OF CLOWNS!

LOOK CLOSER

In Batman: Rescue from Rā's al Ghūl (set 76056), anti-hero Talia al Ghūl has carved "B+T" (Batman and Talia) in a heart shape on the wall of a hideout.

WORST DRESSED?

Trickster

3

bad guys so big they don't fit into minifigure form: Gorilla Grodd, Killer Croc, and Darkseid!

CALL ME "LOCKS LUTHOR"!

REALLY?!

Lex Luthor battles Superman in six sets, but only in Heroes of Justice: Sky-High Battle (set 76046) does he have any hair.

CLAWS OUT

Catwoman isn't the only feline foe in the DC Super Heroes universe. In 2020, Batman did battle with Bronze Tiger, while Wonder Woman went to war with Cheetah!

LOOK CLOSER

Harleen Quinzel might look like a friendly doctor, but under her white coat you can see the red and black outfit of villainous Harley Quinn!

WOW!

Green Lantern's alien enemy Sinestro is the first minifigure ever to have a bright purple head!

NO, I'M NOT HOLDING MY BREATH.

Top 5

LEGO villains based on the 1960s *Batman* TV series

1. The Joker
2. The Riddler
3. Mr. Freeze
4. The Penguin
5. Catwoman

The Joker

Mr Freeze

The Riddler

The Penguin

Catwoman

Piece particulars

Shark pieces have been around since 1989, but only in the LEGO DC Super Heroes theme do they come in black – and with lasers added by Aquaman's enemy, Black Manta!

IT'S A SIGN!

Batzarro is a mixed-up monster version of Batman, created by Lex Luthor. He wears the Caped Crusader's famous symbol on his chest but, like his Utility Belt, it is upside down.

Special scale LEGO® figures

1 **DUPLO dolls.** Four large LEGO DUPLO dolls with realistic proportions and fabric clothes were released in 2001. Standing about 18 bricks high, each doll came with its own, much smaller, doll toy that was slightly larger than a LEGO minifigure.

2 **SCALA dolls.** The largest and most realistic of all LEGO figures, LEGO® SCALA dolls stood more than 15.2 cm (6 in) tall, wore fabric clothes, and had brushable hair. The dolls featured in more than 40 sets between 1997 and 2001.

3 **LEGO Technic figures.** The first LEGO Technic figures braved the cold in Arctic-themed sets from 1986. Looking like taller, more athletic minifigures, they appeared in 36 sets in 28 variations – including scary cyborgs!

4 **BELVILLE figures.** Twice the height of a minifigure, each BELVILLE figure had 14 points of articulation – more than any other LEGO figure. Launched in 1994, the theme also included baby figures and, later, small fairies without any articulation.

ALL SHAPES AND SIZES

5   **Fabuland figures**. More than 20 animal species inhabited the Fabuland world between 1979 and 1989. They all shared the same articulated body shape and included crocodiles, hippos, and walruses.

6   **DUPLO figures**. In 1977, the first LEGO DUPLO figures had chunky single-block bodies and heads that turned but didn't come off. By 1983, some DUPLO figures had moving arms and legs, but still no removable parts for safety reasons.

7   *Basic* **figures.** LEGO Basic figures came in two variations between 1981 and 1991: blue and red. Their hollow bodies meant they could be used as finger puppets, and they were the first LEGO figures to have noses!

CHAPTER FIVE

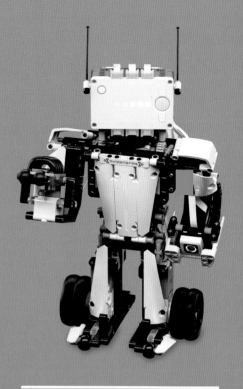

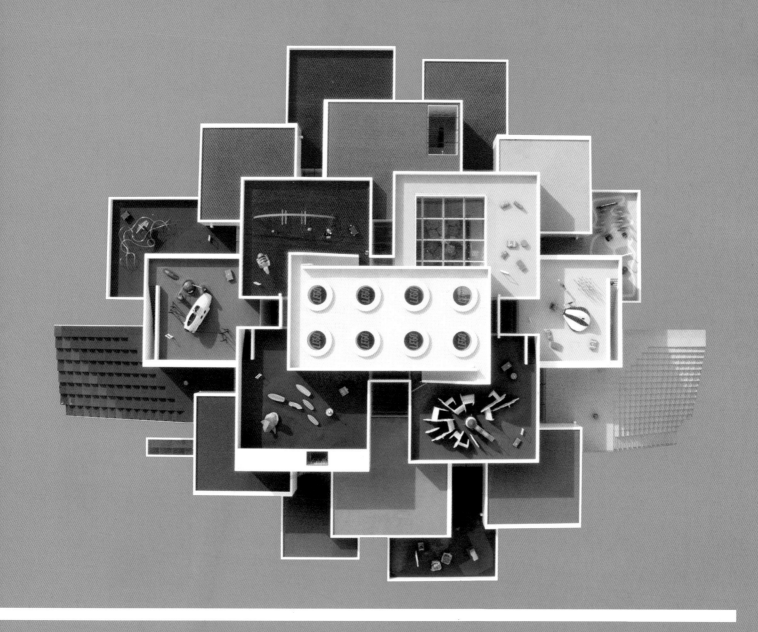

BEYOND
THE BRICK

FACT STACK

The LEGO Group was founded by master carpenter and joiner Ole Kirk Kristiansen.

Ole Kirk ran the company until 1957, when his son, Godtfred Kirk Christiansen, took over.

In 1979, Ole Kirk's grandson, Kjeld Kirk Kristiansen, was made chief executive officer.

Today, the LEGO Group is jointly owned by Kjeld Kirk and his three children.

REALLY?!

In its early days as a wooden toy manufacturer, the LEGO Group also made ladders and ironing boards!

Ole, Godtfred, and Kjeld Kirk Kristiansen together in 1951.

KEY DATES

1891
Ole Kirk Kristiansen is born in Omvrå, in the å Blåhøj-Filskov region of Denmark (not far from Billund), on 7th April.

1903
Ole Kirk becomes an apprentice carpenter and joiner, learning skills from his brother Kristian Bonde Kristiansen in Give, Denmark.

1916
After completing his apprenticeship and military service, Ole Kirk buys a joinery factory in the rural community of Billund.

1924
Wood shavings in Ole Kirk's workshop catch fire, causing the workshop and the family home to burn down. Work starts on rebuilding a new house (pictured).

1932
A global economic crisis threatens Ole Kirk's rebuilt business. With no other carpentry work available, he begins to make wooden toys.

1934
Ole Kirk holds a competition among his employees to name his growing company. He wins it himself by devising the LEGO® name!

Q Why are Ole Kirk Kristiansen and Godtfred Kirk Christiansen's surnames spelled differently?

A Both were born "Kristiansen", but it was common to use both spellings interchangeably. Ole Kirk used both versions, but kept "Kristiansen" on his birth certificate, while Godtfred officially changed to the "Ch" spelling in the 1980s.

IT'S A SIGN!

DET·BEDSTE·ER
IKKE·FOR·GODT

When Ole Kirk Kristiansen coined the LEGO Group motto "Only the best is good enough" in 1936, his son Godtfred Kirk Christiansen turned it into a woodcut for the wall of their workshop.

WOW!

Ole Kirk Kristiansen came up with the LEGO name by combining the Danish words "leg godt" meaning "play well".

Brick History

In 1942, fire destroyed the LEGO factory. Though his life's work was lost, Ole Kirk Kristiansen set about building a new factory – the birthplace of the LEGO plastic brick.

The house and workshop Ole Kirk Kristiansen built in 1924 still stands in Billund, and has even been made into a LEGO set.

10

The number of employees who worked at the LEGO factory in 1939.

PLASTIC PIONEER

Ole Kirk Kristiansen was among the first to see the potential of plastic toys. An early success was a model tractor in 1952. Though expensive to make, the tractor turned a healthy profit, which helped him to further develop another product: plastic bricks.

WHERE IT ALL BEGAN

The worldwide success of the LEGO Group can all be traced back to one man in a workshop in Billund, Denmark, where the company still has its headquarters today.

BRICK BEGINNINGS

LEGO® bricks get to be spaceships, sports cars, castles, and more – but there's another amazing journey they all go on first!

1 LEGO bricks start out as small plastic granules called granulate, each one smaller than a grain of rice. The Billund factory, Kornmarken, can get through 90 tonnes (102 tons) of granulate per day.

2 Powerful vacuum pumps suck the granulate out of huge metal silos and whiz it through pipes into moulding machines. Every factory has many miles of pipes and several hundred moulding machines.

3 When it reaches the machinery, the granulate is melted into a thick, gooey liquid at temperatures ranging from 230°C to 310°C (446°F to 590°F) – that's up to three times hotter than boiling water.

4 The liquid plastic is injected into a metal mould and instantly starts to cool. To make sure it forms a perfect brick, it is subjected to pressure of up to 1 tonne per cm² (7.1 tons per square inch). This is equal to 0.6–0.9 tonnes per square metre for a 2×4 brick.

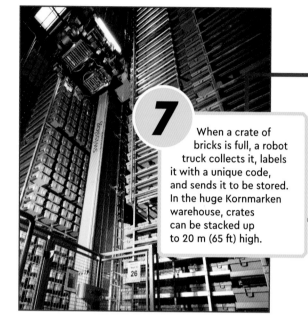

7 When a crate of bricks is full, a robot truck collects it, labels it with a unique code, and sends it to be stored. In the huge Kornmarken warehouse, crates can be stacked up to 20 m (65 ft) high.

6 During quality testing, each LEGO brick is moulded to the accuracy of a hair's width (5my/0.005) to ensure the perfect "clutch power" that holds LEGO creations together.

5 Bricks harden in around 10 to 15 seconds, after which they are ejected from the moulds. They fall onto a conveyor belt and into large crates, then some from each batch are taken for testing.

8 When a crate is needed, a robot crane knows exactly where it is! It confirms what's inside using the unique label, slides the crate out of the stack, and sends it on its way along a conveyor belt.

9 If the bricks in the crate need a printed design on them, such as the vests on these LEGO® City Police minifigure torsos, they are sent to the decoration department.

10 Some parts are put together in the factory, including minifigure legs onto hips and wheels onto tyres. These parts go through their own special assembly machines before they rejoin the main production line.

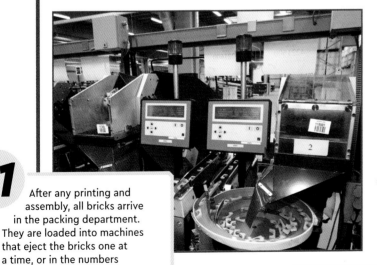

11 After any printing and assembly, all bricks arrive in the packing department. They are loaded into machines that eject the bricks one at a time, or in the numbers needed for a specific set.

15 Robot cranes load the packaged sets onto pallets for distribution by road and by sea. Bricks that were piles of granulate just a short time ago are now on their way to stores and homes around the world!

14 The bags pass down chutes and are placed in the cardboard display boxes they will be sold in. The boxes are checked and sealed by machine, then sealed into larger boxes for delivery.

13 High-precision scales weigh the boxes along the route to make sure no pieces are missing. At the end of the conveyor belt, another machine seals the contents of each small bag.

12 Bricks of different kinds meet for the first time as small boxes pass beneath the packing machines, filling up with the precise selection of parts required as they go along.

BOX CLEVER

The LEGO Group gives its boxes, bags, and tubs the same care and attention that it gives to the LEGO® bricks and models inside the packaging.

Q Do all LEGO sets come in boxes?

A No, not all. There have also been LEGO® BIONICLE® carry canisters, LEGO brick-shaped creative building tubs, and LEGO® DUPLO® sets shaped like everything from aeroplanes to animals.

10,004

Number of pieces contained in the biggest-ever LEGO box. The Ultimate Battle For CHIMA contained 25 LEGO® Legends of Chima™ sets and was the grand prize in a 2015 LEGO Club competition.

TREASURE CHESTS

From 1957 to 1972, some LEGO sets came in large wooden boxes. These are now collector's items – even when they don't have any LEGO bricks in them!

Several LEGO set boxes of the 1950s featured LEGO Group founder Ole Kirk Kristiansen's grandchildren, Hanne, Gunhild, and Kjeld Kirk, playing with the bricks inside.

Brick History

Between 1956 and 1959, the front of LEGO Town Plan boxes featured paintings of the sets inside, along with a friendly figure usually known as the LEGO Gnome.

REALLY?!

In 2008, Kjeld Kirk Kristiansen reprised his role as a LEGO box star for Town Plan (set 10184), celebrating 50 years of the LEGO brick. By this point, Kjeld Kirk was also the owner of the LEGO Group.

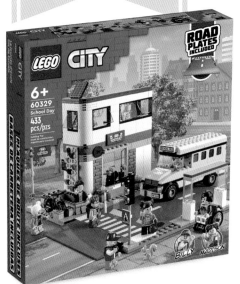

DON'T PUT YOUR FOOT IN IT!

Not every modern LEGO set has a photo of the contents on the outside. The adidas Originals Superstar (set 10282) from 2021 comes in picture-free packaging designed to look like an adidas shoe box!

WOW!

All paper and cardboard used in LEGO products and product packaging is recyclable, sustainably sourced, and certified by the Forest Stewardship Council™.

I MADE THIS

LEGO® Designers put their all into making new sets, so it's no surprise that they sometimes include personal references and nods to their favourite old sets.

Dizzy heights. The nervous-looking minifigure in 2015's LEGO® Creator Expert Ferris Wheel (set 10247) is a joke about Set Designer Jamie Berard's reluctance to ride on the real thing!

Why is she waiting? The LEGO® Minifigures Diner Waitress from 2013 is based on LEGO Designer Tara Wike, and she wears a name badge to prove it.

Written in the stars. Stickers in 2011's LEGO® Space Earth Defence HQ (set 7066) are Set Designer Mark Stafford's tribute to the late Nate Nielsen, a LEGO fan builder known online as "Nnenn".

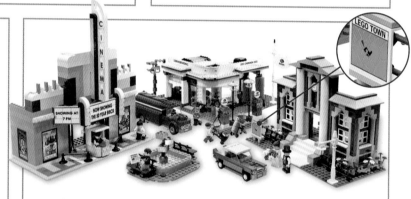

On the map. The "LEGO Town" map in 2008's 50th anniversary LEGO set, Town Plan (set 10184), actually shows where the LEGO Group was founded in Billund, Denmark.

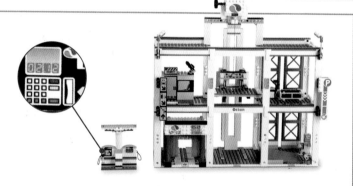

It's a date! The price of gas shown in 2012's City Garage (set 4207) from the LEGO® City theme just happens to be the birth date of Designer Samuel Johnson.

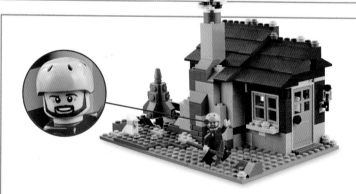

Smiling selfie. The bearded trail biker in the LEGO Creator Mountain Hut (set 31025) from 2014 is a minifigure self-portrait by Set Designer Morten Rauff.

Face of the farm. The farmer in 2009's LEGO City Farm subtheme is based on LEGO Designer Chris Bonveen. When Chris himself came to design a new farmer in 2016, he used the opportunity to show how he had aged in real life!

A familiar face. Designer Matthew Boyle based the banker's portrait in 2016's LEGO Creator Expert Brick Bank (set 10251) on Chris Bonveen (see left). He reasoned that it was a picture of the minifigure farmer's brother!

Pet project. Glurt (set 41519) from 2014's LEGO® Mixels™ range is based on LEGO Set Designer Mark Stafford's dog – only green and much more slimy.

Family affair. Set Designer Jamie Berard based a minifigure in 2009's Winter Toy Shop (set 10199) on his mum, and named Chez Albert in 2014's Parisian Restaurant (set 10243) after his dad.

DUPLO D.O.B. Senior Designer Mette Grue-Sørensen used number plates to personalize her designs. The cars at 2009's LEGO DUPLO Petrol Station (set 5640) and Busy Garage (set 5641) all have her initials and date of birth on the back.

Train tribute. The flight numbers listed on the departure board in 1990's LEGO Town Airport Shuttle (set 6399) are, in fact, set numbers of classic 1980s LEGO® Trains.

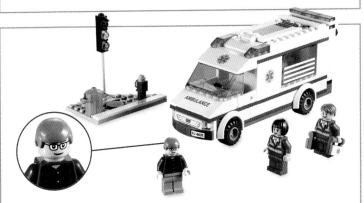

Model mentor. Set Designer Samuel Johnson based the look of the cyclist minifigure in 2012's LEGO City Ambulance (set 4431) on his mentor, LEGO Master Model Coach Torben Skov.

PICTURE PERFECT

Budding artists have always made pictures and patterns from LEGO® parts, but in recent years sets have been especially designed for mosaic makers.

Piece particulars

In 2022, the LEGO® DOTS theme introduced the first ever stick-on and stitch-on LEGO elements. The special 8×8 plates are designed to be decorated and attached to walls and clothing.

IT'S A SIGN!

Some LEGO DOTS elements are artworks in themselves, thanks to their small but perfectly formed prints!

36 designs are included with Art Project – Create Together (set 21226), including a portrait of a classic LEGO Space minifigure!

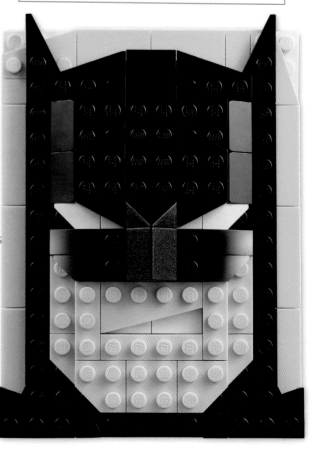

I'M FLATMAN!

WHAT A RELIEF

LEGO artists looking to create on a smaller canvas can turn to the Brick Sketches theme. These postcard-sized LEGO plate portraits have depicted cool characters such as Batman (set 40386) since 2020.

AWESOME!
The LEGO DOTS Big Message Board (set 41952) is designed for spelling out any message you like, with captions up to 50 cm (20 in) wide!

Q Why is there a LEGO® Art set in the shape of a giant tongue?!

A That's the long-time logo of rock band The Rolling Stones (set 31206)! It was released to mark the band's 60th anniversary in 2022, and is the first LEGO Art set not to be square or rectangular.

FACT STACK

The first LEGO Art set was a version of pop artist Andy Warhol's Marilyn Monroe (set 31197) in 2020.

LEGO DOTS also launched in 2020, using small and colourful LEGO tiles to make home and fashion accessories.

To date, there have been more than 70 DOTS sets, including more than 20 customizable bracelets.

WOW!

Upload a selfie at LEGO.com and you can order a Personalised Mosaic Portrait (set 40179) made from 4,502 pieces!

AWESOME!

Combining three copies of *Star Wars: The Sith* (set 31200) can create a 116 cm (46 in) image of Darth Vader made from almost 7,000 pieces!

LEGO® LIFESTYLE

LEGO® sets have always had display potential, but in recent years, several large-scale builds have been released specifically as ornaments and lifestyle statements.

The 2020 **Orchid** (set 10281) is part of the LEGO Botanical Collection, a range of life-sized, lifelike plant builds – ideal for people who forget to water their flowers!

Since 2020, LEGO® *Star Wars™* Helmet Collection sets such as **Stormtrooper Helmet** (set 75276) have given fans a new way to show off their favourite franchise!

Old Trafford – Manchester United (set 10272) from 2021 is the first of a series of huge brick-built sports arenas suited to football fans with space to spare!

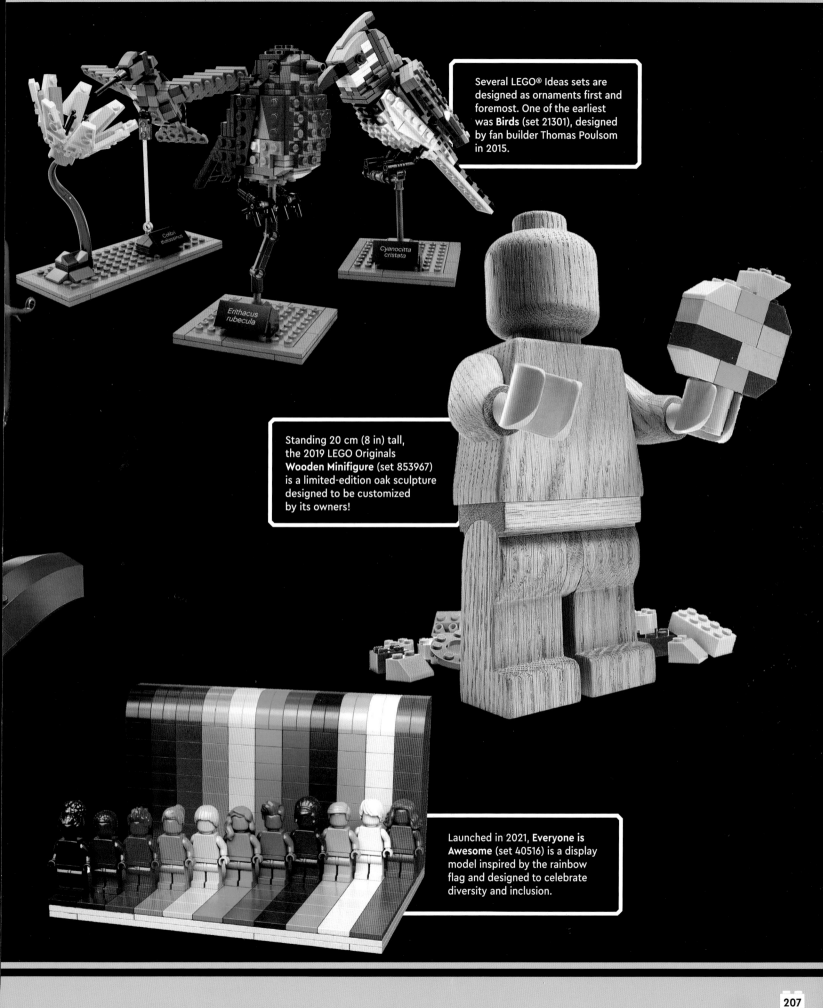

Several LEGO® Ideas sets are designed as ornaments first and foremost. One of the earliest was **Birds** (set 21301), designed by fan builder Thomas Poulsom in 2015.

Standing 20 cm (8 in) tall, the 2019 LEGO Originals **Wooden Minifigure** (set 853967) is a limited-edition oak sculpture designed to be customized by its owners!

Launched in 2021, **Everyone is Awesome** (set 40516) is a display model inspired by the rainbow flag and designed to celebrate diversity and inclusion.

Colibri thalassinus

Cyanocitta cristata

Erithacus rubecula

FAN-TASTIC IDEAS

Thanks to the LEGO® Ideas theme, LEGO fan builders can now see their coolest creations turned into official LEGO sets for everyone to enjoy!

LOOK CLOSER

Classic LEGO Pirates® captain Redbeard returns in 2020's LEGO Pirates of Barracuda Bay (set 21322), where time has turned his famous facial hair grey!

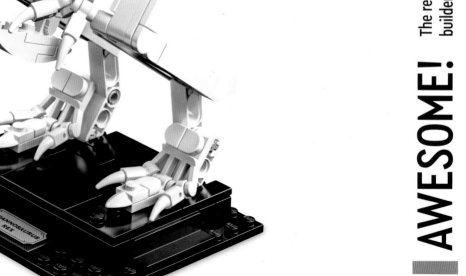

FACT STACK

LEGO Ideas started out as LEGO CUUSOO, a website for LEGO fans in Japan, in 2008.

"Cuusoo" is a Japanese word meaning "imagination" and can also mean "wish".

LEGO CUUSOO launched around the world in 2011 and became LEGO Ideas in 2014.

The realistic T rex skeleton in Dinosaur Fossils (set 21320, designed by fan builder Jonathan Brunn) is more than 40 cm (16 in) long from teeth to tail!

AWESOME!

Q How do I submit an idea for a new LEGO set?

A If you are aged 13 or older, you can create a LEGO Ideas profile, submit your own ideas, and support others at ideas.LEGO.com.

LARGEST LEGO IDEAS SET

A 3,995-piece version of the house from the movie Home Alone!

REALLY?!

Andrew Clark, the fan designer behind Doctor Who (set 21304), is the nephew of Paul McGann – the eighth actor to play the Doctor in the BBC sci-fi series.

ROLE-MODEL MAKING

LEGO fan builder Ellen Kooijman designed 2014's Research Institute (set 21110) to inspire girls to become anything they want to be – including paleontologists, chemists, and astronomers.

WOW!

Designed by fan Guillaume Roussel, this glorious globe (set 21332) measures 82 cm (32 in) around the equator, really spins, and has glow-in-the-dark labels!

10,000

The number of supporters a project needs before being considered by the LEGO Review Board as a possible set.

EVERYTHING IS AWESOME

Brick History

Spaceman Benny was based on one particular minifigure that Chris Miller (one of THE LEGO MOVIE writer/directors) has owned since childhood, right down to his worn-out printing and broken helmet.

Minifigures became movie stars in 2014's THE LEGO® MOVIE™. Its success soon led to the return of heroes Emmet and Lucy in THE LEGO® MOVIE 2™: The Second Part!

WOW!

THE LEGO MOVIE 2 is the only play theme to combine LEGO minifigures with LEGO mini dolls such as Sweet Mayhem.

4

different versions of the infectious theme song, Everything is AWESOME!!!, feature on THE LEGO MOVIE soundtrack. AWESOME!!!

BIG NAME MINIFIGURE

The star of THE LEGO MOVIE and its sequel is Emmet Brickowski, a construction worker minifigure voiced by Chris Pratt. Minifigures based on the actor's other film roles can be found in the LEGO® Marvel Super Heroes and Jurassic World themes.

Piece particulars

Lord Business's cape is actually a life-sized businessman's tie! Towards the end of THE LEGO MOVIE, "the Man Upstairs" can be seen wearing one in the same colour.

FACT STACK

Everything you see in THE LEGO MOVIE and its sequel was built using digital versions of real LEGO bricks.

Animators added scratches, teeth-marks, and fingerprints to make the digital bricks look like real-life toys.

More than 60 sets were released based on THE LEGO MOVIE and THE LEGO MOVIE 2 between 2014 and 2019.

REALLY?!

Two years before Batman v Superman: Dawn of Justice, THE LEGO MOVIE was the first time Batman and Superman appeared together on the big screen.

AWESOME!

As well as having 14 minifigure variants, Lucy Wyldstyle has also been made as a LEGO DUPLO figure and a LEGO® BrickHeadz™ model!

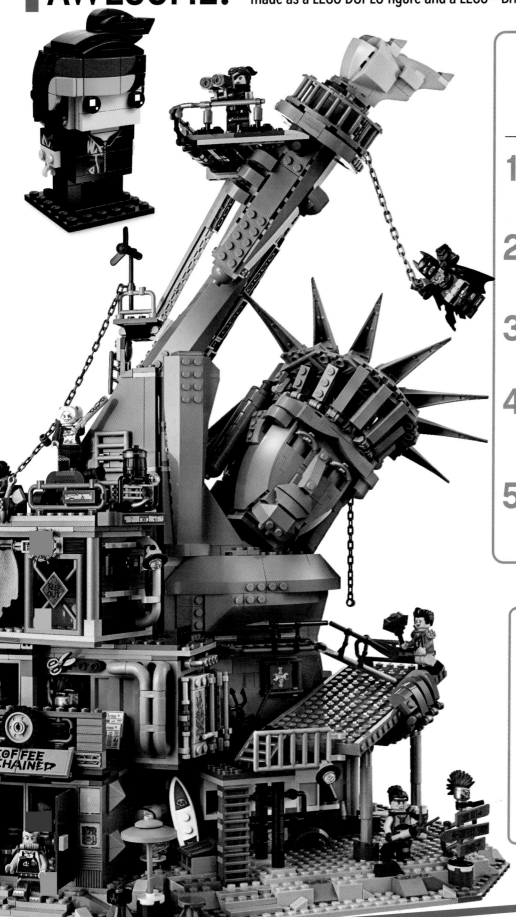

FUN 5

Classic set cameos in THE LEGO MOVIE

1 LEGO Pirates Brickbeard's Bounty (set 6243), 2009

2 LEGO® Castle King's Castle (set 70404), 2013

3 LEGO® Friends Sunshine Ranch (set 41039), 2014

4 LEGO® Fabuland Cathy Cat's Fun Park (set 3676), 1989

5 LEGO® Vikings Viking Ship Challenges the Midgard Serpent (set 7018), 2005

Brick statistics

Welcome to Apocalypseburg! (set 70840)

3,178 pieces
By far the biggest set from THE LEGO MOVIE 2

10 exclusive minifigures
plus Emmet and Lucy, of course!

52 centimetres (20 inches)
from ground level to the tip of the torch

2 green sausages
to make the fallen statue's eyebrows!

BIG-SCREEN BATMAN

Soon after LEGO® Batman made his big-screen debut in THE LEGO® MOVIE™, he got to star in his very own feature – and an array of brand-new Bat-sets!

> I DO ALL MY OWN STUNTS.

FACT STACK

THE LEGO® BATMAN MOVIE had its world premiere in Dublin, Ireland, on 29 January 2017.

More than 30 play sets and two waves of collectible Minifigures based on the film were released in 2017 and 2018.

The film's tagline is "Always be yourself... Unless you can be Batman"!

WOW!

As well as being the voice of LEGO Batman, actor Will Arnett is also the host of the LEGO Masters TV show in the USA!

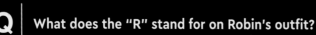

Q What does the "R" stand for on Robin's outfit?

A It may be the first letter of "Robin", but according to THE LEGO BATMAN MOVIE, the Boy Wonder adapted his costume from one of Batman's many disguises – labelled "R" for "Reggae Man"!

❙ AWESOME!

Before he voiced Two-Face in THE LEGO® BATMAN MOVIE, Billy Dee Williams played the villain's good-guy alter ego, Harvey Dent, in 1989's Batman film!

40

collectible minifigures based on THE LEGO BATMAN MOVIE, including Fairy Batman, Glam Metal Batman, and Mermaid Batman!

REALLY?!

Five years before she played Catwoman in 2022's *The Batman*, actor Zoe Kravitz voiced the minifigure-version of the character in THE LEGO BATMAN MOVIE!

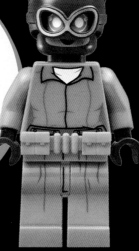

IT'S A SIGN!

A printed dome piece and light brick combine to make the first functional LEGO Bat signal in The Ultimate Batmobile (set 70917)

Piece particulars

Brand-new parts created for THE LEGO BATMAN MOVIE sets include the Penguin's umbrella, a question mark-shaped cane for the Riddler, and the Utility Belt element worn by both Batman and Batgirl.

LOOK CLOSER

Even the box for The Joker Manor (set 70922) has been covered in graffiti by the Clown Prince of Crime!

FUN 5

Special Patrol Vehicles

1 The Ultimate Batmobile (set 70917)

2 The Joker's Notorious Lowrider (set 70906)

3 The Scuttler (set 70908)

4 The Penguin's Arctic Roller (set 70911)

5 The Bat-Space Shuttle (set 70923)

SO NINJA!

Everyone's favourite ninja team spun into cinemas in 2017, with the release of THE LEGO® NINJAGO® MOVIE™. The six Spinjitzu stars all got new looks, along with new friends and updated enemies!

REALLY?!

Highly trained stunt performers tried out all the fight scenes in the movie to make the animated action look believable.

FACT STACK

THE LEGO NINJAGO MOVIE takes a fresh look at the relationship between Green Ninja Lloyd and his villainous dad, Lord Garmadon!

Unlike other LEGO movies, the story does not take place in a world made entirely out of LEGO bricks.

To date, 30 play sets and 20 collectible Minifigures have been based on the movie.

LOOK CLOSER

Several NINJAGO movie minifigures wear clothes showing their love for other LEGO themes – including LEGO Space, THE LEGO MOVIE, and Galidor!

Brick statistics

NINJAGO City (set 70620)

3 detachable levels
linked by a working lift

5 bustling businesses
including a comic shop and a sushi bar

18 NINJAGO MOVIE minifigures
including 15 found in no other sets!

4,857 pieces in 50 different colours
standing more than 63 cm (25 in) high when combined!

FUN 5

Laid-back movie star looks

1 Casual Kai

2 Couch-ready Cole

3 No-worries Nya

4 Away-day Jay

5 Goodnight Garmadon!

Q Does THE LEGO NINJAGO MOVIE make sense if you haven't seen the TV series?

A Yes! The movie is designed to stand apart from the TV series, and makes a great starting point for NINJAGO newbies!

1

Number of real-life cats it takes to trash NINJAGO City in the movie!

JACKIE WHO?

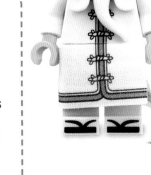

WOW!

Martial arts movie legend Jackie Chan, who plays both Mr Liu and Master Wu in the movie, has appeared in more than 150 films!

Piece particulars

Among the many new pieces created for THE LEGO NINJAGO MOVIE sets were new hairstyles for the ninja and shark-shaped helmets for Garmadon's goons!

COMICS

STARS OF THE SMALL SCREEN

From Fabuland to Freya McCloud, NINJAGO ninja to NEXO KNIGHTS heroes, LEGO® characters have a long history of coming to life on TV, DVD, and online!

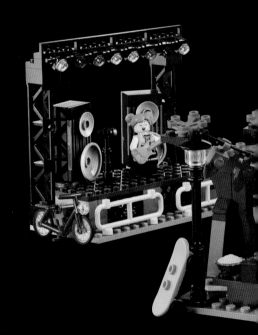

12

variants of Unikitty released with her self-titled TV series in 2018 – including one dressed as a dinosaur!

RAWR!

Q What was the first-ever LEGO TV show?

A Way back in 1987, the animals of LEGO Fabuland were made into clay figures for the stop-motion animated series *Edward and Friends*. It starred Edward the Elephant... and his friends!

FACT STACK

The first computer-generated LEGO animation was a 2003 LEGO® BIONICLE® DVD movie.

LEGO *Star Wars* made its TV debut in the animated short film *Revenge of the Brick* on Cartoon Network in 2005.

Themes with their own animated series include LEGO Legends of Chima, LEGO® Hidden Side, LEGO® NEXO KNIGHTS™, and LEGO Friends.

Brick statistics

LEGO NINJAGO

210 regular episodes
since 2011, divided into 15 seasons and one miniseries

4 pilot episodes
introducing the ninja for the first time

6 mini-episodes
set between the pilots and season one

5 YouTube specials
to celebrate 10 years of NINJAGO

1 TV special
The 2016 epic *Day of the Departed*

60 hours
the time it would take to watch it all!

MEET THE FREEMAKERS

In 2016, LEGO *Star Wars: The Freemaker Adventures* was the first LEGO *Star Wars* TV series to focus on brand-new characters, rather than familiar faces from the movie saga. Four LEGO sets featured starships designed exclusively for the series.

MOST MONSTROUS MINISERIES

LEGO® Jurassic World: Legend of Isla Nublar (2019)

I'M A BREAKOUT STAR!

CITY SETS

Since 2019, many LEGO City sets have included named characters from the hit LEGO *City Adventures* TV series. Main Square (set 60271) includes six small-screen stars among its 15 minifigures!

AWESOME!

To date, the animated LEGO® Monkie Kid™ series and its one-off specials have been seen by more than 900 million people in China alone!

WOW!

Though the LEGO® DC Comics Super Heroes have never had their own TV series, they have starred in more than a dozen TV and DVD specials!

BRICKS AND PIXELS

LEGO® video games combine timeless LEGO play and familiar minifigures with huge virtual worlds that could never be built in real life.

3,200,000

copies of LEGO *Star Wars: The Skywalker Saga* for Windows, Nintendo Switch, PlayStation, and Xbox were sold in its first two weeks of release in 2022!

FIRST MINIFIGURE BASED ON A GAME

Infomaniac (set 2181), 1997

COME WITH ME TO LEGO ISLAND!

KEY DATES

1997
LEGO® *Island* is the first ever LEGO PC game. On the island, players can build vehicles and meet friendly minifigures.

1999
LEGO® *Racers* was the first LEGO game released for several different games consoles, and features motor-racing pirates, knights, and aliens.

2005
LEGO *Star Wars: The Video Game* takes LEGO gaming to a new level, with a storyline spanning the entire *Star Wars* prequel trilogy.

2008
LEGO *Batman: The Video Game* is the first licensed LEGO game to tell an original story, rather than adapting a movie plot.

2010
LEGO® *Universe* becomes the first LEGO multiplayer online game. In it, players use their building skills to save imagination itself.

WOW!

The LEGO Minifigures Gingerbread Man is a playable character in 2015's LEGO NINJAGO: Shadow of Ronin video game!

I'M A GINGER NINJA!

DUNK ME!

LOOK CLOSER

LEGO UNIVERSE

The "U" in the logo for 2010's LEGO *Universe* game is a minifigure hand viewed from above.

Brick statistics

Batman 3: Beyond Gotham (2014)

32 voice actors
including 1960s Batman actor Adam West

150 built-in characters
plus another 70 available for download

45 missions
including zero-gravity outer-space action

28 playable vehicles
plus 10 more available for download

8 Batsuits
including Arctic, Space, and Scuba suits

AWESOME!

The playable world of 2014's THE LEGO MOVIE game was built entirely from virtual LEGO bricks – making it technically possible to build the game world in real life!

FACT STACK

The first LEGO video game was LEGO® *Fun To Build*, released for the Sega Pico console in 1995.

Other early games included LEGO® *Chess* and city-building simulator LEGO® *Loco*.

Today, there are dozens of LEGO mini-games to play for free on LEGO.com

Q Who were the stars of LEGO® Dimensions?

A Almost everyone! Characters from THE LEGO MOVIE, DC Comics, The Lord of the Rings, Harry Potter, The Simpsons, and more all joined in with the adventure!

Brick History

In 2015, LEGO Dimensions (pictured) combined real-world LEGO sets with video gaming for the first time. Players used a special "Toy Pad" platform to connect their builds with the in-game world.

REALLY?!

In 2017, the LEGO Worlds game offered players an infinite collection of virtual LEGO bricks for building without any limits!

SMART BUILDING

LEGO® MINDSTORMS®, LEGO® BOOST, and LEGO® SPIKE sets blend LEGO building and computer programming to create real-life robots, inspiring endless inventions from young engineers.

Piece particulars

The LEGO MINDSTORMS hub is both a programmable microcomputer and a LEGO building element. It has a built-in speaker and a screen that can be programmed to show a smiley face!

FUN 5

Robots that can be made with LEGO MINDSTORMS Robot Inventor (set 51515)

1 **Charlie**, the drumming and dancing droid.

2 **Tricky**, a bot built for ball games.

3 **Blast**, the missile-launching mega build!

4 **M.V.P.** can be a car, a crane, and more!

5 **Gelo**, a four-legged marching machine!

WOW!

LEGO MINDSTORMS is in the Carnegie Mellon University Robot Hall of Fame, alongside robots such as C-3PO, R2-D2, and WALL-E!

KEY DATES

1984
The LEGO Group partners with the Massachusetts Institute of Technology Media Laboratory to develop educational computer-controlled LEGO sets for schools.

1998
The LEGO MINDSTORMS Robotics Invention System (set 9719) introduces the programmable RCX (Robotic Command eXplorer) brick for building working robots!

2006
LEGO MINDSTORMS NXT (set 8527) makes LEGO robotics more powerful, but also easier to use, using the NXT Intelligent Brick.

2013
LEGO MINDSTORMS EV3 (set 31313) takes LEGO programming to the next level, with complete control from your smartphone or tablet.

3.253

seconds taken by LEGO MINDSTORMS robot Cubestormer III to solve a Rubik's Cube.

REALLY?!

In 2014, 12-year-old Shubham Banerjee used LEGO MINDSTORMS EV3 to build Braigo – the world's lightest, quietest, most cost-effective braille printer!

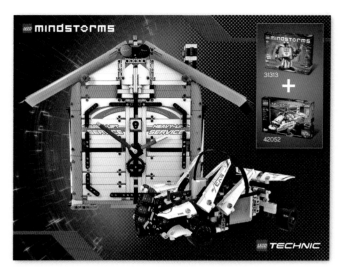

AWESOME!

You can build a working cuckoo clock by combining LEGO MINDSTORMS EV3 (set 31313) with 2016's LEGO Technic Heavy Lift Helicopter (set 42052).

Brick statistics

LEGO MINDSTORMS Robot Inventor (set 51515)

949 LEGO elements
for building robots up to 26 cm (10 in) tall!

4 compact motors
for powerful, precise movement

2 smart sensors
detect distance and different colours

1 rechargeable hub
the "brain" of your MINDSTORMS robot!

FACT STACK

LEGO MINDSTORMS robots are programmed with a free and easy-to-use LEGO app.

LEGO SPIKE is the LEGO Education version of MINDSTORMS, used in schools around the world.

LEGO MINDSTORMS is the best-selling product in the history of the LEGO Group!

A LEAGUE OF THEIR OWN

In 2008, the LEGO Group and educational charity FIRST (For Inspiration and Recognition of Science and Technology) launched a LEGO MINDSTORMS competition for school students. Today, the *FIRST* LEGO® League has more than 32,000 school teams worldwide.

2017
LEGO BOOST (set 17101) brings coding to a younger audience with buildable, programmable characters such as Vernie the Robot and Frankie the Cat.

2020
New for schools, LEGO SPIKE introduces new tech also found in the fourth generation of LEGO MINDSTORMS for use at home.

221

REALLY?!

One of the coolest parts of LEGO headquarters in Billund is the LEGO Archive, where almost every LEGO set ever made is kept in its original box!

FUN 5

Attractions at the world's largest LEGO Store in Leicester Square, London

1 Snap a selfie with **William Shakespeare** at the bus stop.

2 Flag down a 270,884-piece **double decker London bus**.

281,786+

people visited the LEGO® House in Billund during 2019!

A WORLD OF DISCOVERY

LEGOLAND® Discovery Centres are indoor attractions with rides, building areas, 4-D cinema shows, and more. There are Discovery Centres in Germany, Turkey, the UK, China, Japan, Canada, and Australia – plus 14 in the USA alone.

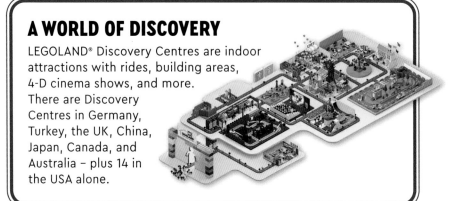

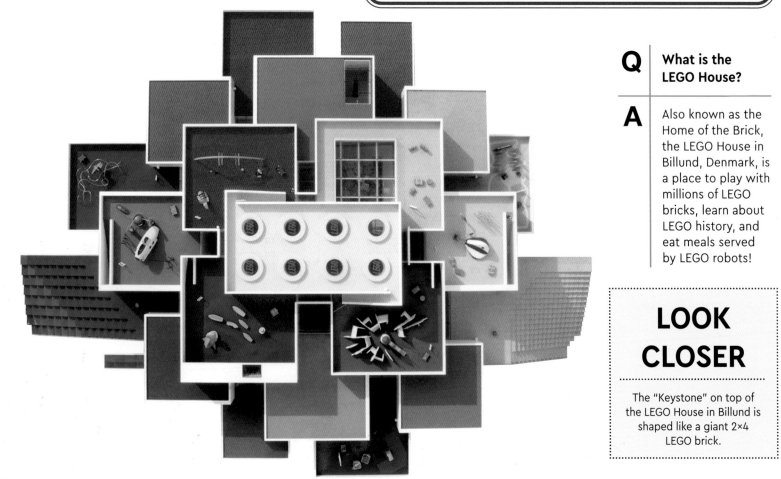

Q What is the LEGO House?

A Also known as the Home of the Brick, the LEGO House in Billund, Denmark, is a place to play with millions of LEGO bricks, learn about LEGO history, and eat meals served by LEGO robots!

LOOK CLOSER

The "Keystone" on top of the LEGO House in Billund is shaped like a giant 2×4 LEGO brick.

3 Take a peek inside the magical **Tree of Discovery**.

4 See LEGO history in the **Storytelling Zone**.

5 Create your own minifigure in the **Personalization Studio!**

The LEGO Group sometimes makes micro-scale models of its factories as gifts for the LEGO loving people who work in them!

Brick History

The first LEGO factory outside Denmark opened in Switzerland in 1974. By 2024, LEGO factories will be found in Denmark, Hungary, Mexico, Czech Republic, China, and Vietnam!

Brick statistics

The LEGO factory in Vietnam (opens 2024)

50 football fields
would fit inside the 44-hectare (109-acre) site

4,000 LEGO colleagues
will eventually work at the facility

50,000 trees
to be planted as part of construction plans

100% renewable energy usage
made possible by a brand new solar farm

LEGO
4000018
Kladno 2015
Campus

FACT STACK

The first LEGO Store opened in Bloomington, Minnesota, in the USA in 1992.

LEGO Group HQ is still based in Billund, Denmark, where the company was founded.

Every LEGO office around the world is stocked with bowls of bricks for staff to play with!

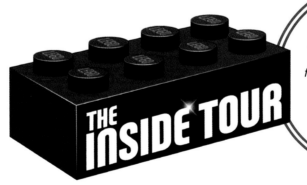

THE INSIDE TOUR

WOW!

Every year, a few lucky fans get to see inside the LEGO factory in Billund as part of the LEGO Inside Tour.

COME ON IN

Not all LEGO® buildings are made from plastic bricks! There are also the factories, stores, offices, and visitor centres found in various locations around the world.

IT'S A LEGOLAND® WORLD!

The first LEGOLAND® Park opened in Billund, Denmark, in 1968. Less than 50 years later, there are now 11 LEGOLAND destinations in three continents.

WOW!

Three new LEGOLAND Parks are set to open in China by 2024, one of which will become the world's largest!

LEGOLAND NEW YORK
United States, opened 2021

Currently the biggest LEGOLAND Resort in the world!

LEGOLAND CALIFORNIA
United States, opened 1999

Home to the world's first LEGOLAND Water Park.

LEGOLAND FLORIDA
United States, opened 2011

Incorporates a botanical garden that has stood on the site since 1936.

Brick statistics

LEGO® MYTHICA: World of Mythical Creatures at LEGOLAND WINDSOR

25 metres (82 feet)
Height of the Flight of the Sky Lion ride

685,530 LEGO bricks
used to build Maximus the mighty Sky Lion

8,649 hours
Time taken to make all 13 mythical creatures

4 heads
on the colossal Chimera creature!

THE LEGO GLOBE

The 11 LEGOLAND parks are spread around the world, each with something special to see.

AWESOME!

Many rooms in LEGOLAND hotels contain a locked safe with LEGO treasures inside – and clues for cracking the code!

REALLY?!

The original Traffic School cars in LEGOLAND Billund ran from 1968 to 2015 before they needed to be replaced.

55,000,000+

visitors to LEGOLAND Billund since it opened in 1968.

LEGOLAND DEUTSCHLAND

Germany, opened 2002

See it all from the 50 m (164 ft) observation tower.

LEGOLAND BILLUND

Denmark, opened 1968

The first LEGOLAND has trebled in size since it opened.

LEGOLAND WATER PARK GARDALAND

Italy, opened 2021

The newest part of the long-established Gardaland resort.

LEGOLAND KOREA

South Korea, opened 2022

The first LEGOLAND Park on a river island!

LEGOLAND JAPAN

Japan, opened 2017

A day at this park starts with a LEGO factory tour.

LEGOLAND WINDSOR

United Kingdom, opened 1996

Built with more than 80 million LEGO bricks.

LEGOLAND DUBAI

United Arab Emirates, opened 2016

The only LEGOLAND Resort with an indoor MINILAND.

LEGOLAND MALAYSIA

Malaysia, opened 2012

The first LEGOLAND Resort to open in Asia.

225

COMMUNITY BUILDING

Since the 1960s, official LEGO® Clubs have connected builders around the world. Today, the community comes together on the LEGO® Life app and on LEGO websites.

Brick History

In 1959, the LEGO Group in Germany launched the LEGO Post newsletter – a fact-packed forerunner of the modern LEGO *Life* magazine!

Brick statistics

14 million likes
on the official LEGO Facebook page

14.8 million subscribers
to the official LEGO YouTube channel

8.4 million followers
of @LEGO on Instagram

942,000 followers
of @LEGO_Group on Twitter

FUN 5

Former LEGO Club cartoon mascots

1 Max (2007)

2 The Amazing Redini (2002)

3 Zack the LEGO Maniac (1989)

4 Brick and Bridget Bildmore (1987)

AWESOME!

In 2022, superstars including Alicia Keys and Thierry Henry took 90-second building challenges on the LEGO YouTube channel to celebrate 90 Years of Play!

*You have to be 13 or older to use most third-party social media sites

FACT STACK

The LEGO Life app is packed full of building challenges, videos, quizzes, polls, and more.

Builders can share photos of their creations in the app without posting any personal info.

User comments in the app are posted entirely in the positive language of LEGO emoji!

IT'S A SIGN!

Click on the games controller icon on LEGO.com to play more than 20 web games, such as LEGO City Builder and LEGO NINJAGO: Golden Legacy!

Q Are there LEGO clubs for older builders?

A Yes, there are adult fan communities all around the world. The oldest such "LEGO User Group" is De Bouwsteen ("The Building Block") in the Netherlands.

people visited LEGO.com in 2020, to do everything from playing games and downloading building instructions to buying individual elements using the Pick a Brick service.

5 Johnny and Jane LEGO (1963)

READ ALL ABOUT IT!

Over the years, LEGO Club magazines have included *Brick Kicks*, *Bricks 'n Pieces*, LEGO *Mania Magazine*, and *Tech Torque* (especially for LEGO® Technic fans). Today, the LEGO *Life* magazine is published four times a year.

1

THE ART OF

2

3

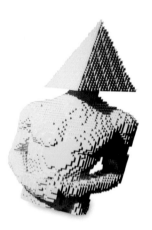

4

Notable LEGO® artists around the world

1 **Paul Hetherington** won the Best
in Show award at LEGO fan event
BrickCon 2015 for his mechanical
"steampunk love story" sculpture,
"Unchain My Heart".

2 **Vesa Lehtimäki** uses sets and
minifigures from the LEGO
Star Wars theme to compose
photographs full of action,
wit, and atmosphere.

3 Since 2004, **Nathan Sawaya** has
worked as a full-time LEGO artist, and
has toured the world with his
exhibition "The Art of the Brick".

4 "Dispatchwork" is a collaborative
art project devised by **Jan Vormann**
in which LEGO bricks are used
to fill cracks and voids in
damaged walls.

5 In 2012, street artist **Megx** painted a
disused rail bridge in Wuppertal,
Germany, to look as if it were made
from giant LEGO bricks.

6 "The Collectivity Project" is a touring
art installation by **Olafur Eliasson.**
It invites visitors to rebuild a
vast LEGO city according to
their own vision.

BUILDING

5

6

7

8

7 **Mike Doyle** builds elaborate, tumbledown LEGO houses, which he photographs for limited-edition art prints before taking them apart and starting again.

8 **Sean Kenney** is a professional artist who creates LEGO sculpture. His latest exhibition, "Nature Connects", features more than 100 lifelike LEGO animals and plants.

RECORD-BREAKING BRICKS

There really are no limits when it comes to LEGO® building, as these remarkable record setters and smashers all set out to show!

The **longest LEGO brick sculpture** ever made was a 1,579 m (5,180 ft) millipede built out of 2,901,760 bricks over the course of two months in 2005. Thousands of families contributed to the creepy-crawly at a shopping centre in Italy, in an event organized by Consorzio Esercenti CC.

LONGEST LEGO SCULPTURE

FASTEST BRICK STACK

The world record for **most LEGO bricks built onto a baseplate** in 30 seconds is currently 140 bricks. Italy's Silvio Sabba beat his own previous record of 130 bricks in November 2018. How many bricks can you add to a baseplate in just 30 seconds?

AM I TOO LATE TO JOIN?

In April 2019, the LEGO Group beat its own world record for the **largest display of minifigures** when it arranged 36,440 stormtroopers in the shape of a stormtrooper helmet at a fan event in Chicago. The display took 12 people around 38 hours to create and measured 6 m² (20 sq ft).

LARGEST MINIFIGURE DISPLAY

In May 2013, the record for the world's **longest LEGO railway** was set by Henrik Ludvigsen and more than 80 other LEGO fans in Denmark. It took a battery-powered LEGO train almost four hours to travel the 4 km (2.5 mile) route, which was made from more than 93,000 LEGO elements!

LONGEST RAILWAY TRACK

LARGEST LEGO SCULPTURE

Standing 13 m (43 ft) high and 44 m (144 ft) wide, a giant model of London's Tower Bridge became the world's **largest LEGO brick sculpture** in September 2016. A year in the planning, it took 28 builders a total of seven months to construct the 5,805,846-piece landmark.

The world's **largest LEGO house** was assembled in the UK by 1,200 volunteers as part of a BBC TV series in 2009. The finished two-storey structure had four life-sized rooms, including a kitchen and a bathroom, and stood 4.6 m (15 ft) tall.

LARGEST LEGO HOUSE

TALLEST LEGO TOWER

The LEGO Group broke its own world record for building the **tallest LEGO tower** in 2015! Around 18,000 volunteers contributed to the 35 m (114 ft) tower in Italy, which comprised more than half a million bricks. The tower took five days to complete, and was built to raise money for an environmental charity.

BUILDING FOR THE FUTURE

With great creativity comes great responsibility! That's why the LEGO Group, through environmental and educational activities, is doing its part in creating a better, brighter world for our children to inherit.

LEGO

Age 0+

031102021

Building Instructions for a Better World

Build the Change

LEGO® EDUCATION

Schools have used LEGO bricks as learning aids for almost as long as there have been LEGO bricks! So, in 1980, the LEGO Group set up LEGO Education as a way to help teachers and children make the most of them. Today, LEGO Education seeks to inspire the curiosity, confidence, and creativity that will prepare the next generation for an ever-changing world.

Plants from plants

In 2018, the LEGO Group started making elements from bio-polyethylene using sustainably sourced sugarcane. Making botanical-themed elements like leaves, bushes, and trees first seemed only natural! This has since been expanded to more than 150 LEGO elements from bio-PE, including many of the LEGO Minifigure accessories.

Q What would you like world leaders to do to take better care of our planet?

A Good question! That's why the LEGO Group put it to more than 6,000 children in 2021 and turned their answers into a 10-step booklet called *Building Instructions for a Better World*. The booklet was then presented at that year's United Nations climate change conference, also known as COP26.

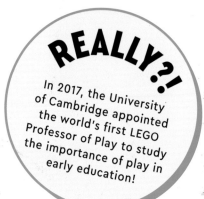

REALLY?!

In 2017, the University of Cambridge appointed the world's first LEGO Professor of Play to study the importance of play in early education!

FUN 5

LEGO Education strands

1 **BricQ** brings physical science to life without batteries or motors.

2 **SPIKE** develops coding skills through fun, programmable LEGO builds.

3 **SPIKE Prime Expansion** set provides exciting robotic challenges!

4 **Early Learning** sets use LEGO DUPLO elements to promote development.

5 **LEGO® Minifigure Collectible Series** help children explore their world through role play.

170,000+

children playing with pre-loved LEGO bricks donated to LEGO® Replay in the US and Canada since 2019. LEGO Replay is a scheme for LEGO fans to pass on their spare bricks to the children who need them most.

Brick History

In 2021, the LEGO Group piloted using paper-based bags inside its sets, instead of plastic ones. The company aims to make all of its packaging more sustainable by the end of 2025.

The LEGO Group has doubled the solar power capacity in its factories and recently announced the construction of two new carbon-neutral factories in Vietnam and Virginia.

WOW!

The LEGO Creator Modular Modern Home (set 31068) has a solar skylight to gather the Sun's energy. The solar panel powers the LEGO house and a charging station for an electric car, too!

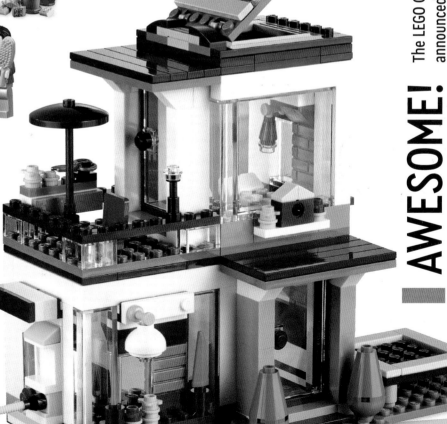

AWESOME!

INDEX

ACKNOWLEDGEMENTS

The publisher would like to thank the following for their kind permission to reproduce their photographs:

Picture library credits:

DK would also like to thank the following people for their help in producing this book:

Signe Wiese, Kristian Reimer Hauge, Camilla Pedersen, Jan Ryaa, and the many designers at the LEGO Group who contributed additional insider facts for this book • Randi Sørensen, Ashley Blais, Nina Koopman, Martin Leighton Lindhardt, and Heidi K. Jensen at the LEGO Group for their roles in bringing this book to fruition • Joel Baker for the use of his LEGOLAND® Florida photography • Jan Vormann, Sean Kenney, Mike Doyle, Megx, Paul Hetherington, and Vesa Lehtimäki for allowing us to feature images of their LEGO® artworks.

Paris

DK | Penguin Random House

Senior Editor **Elizabeth Cook**
Senior Designer **Lauren Adams**
Designer **Elena Jarmoskaite**
Production Editor **Siu Yin Chan**
Senior Production Controller **Lloyd Robertson**
Managing Editor **Paula Regan**
Managing Art Editor **Jo Connor**
Publisher **Mark Searle**

DK would like to thank the author Simon Hugo, and additional writers
Rod Gillies and Caylin Malloy. Also Vanessa Bird for proofreading
and index creation.

First published in Great Britain in 2023 by
Dorling Kindersley Limited
DK, One Embassy Gardens, 8 Viaduct Gardens,
London SW11 7BW
Previous edition published in 2017
as LEGO *Absolutely Everything You Need to Know*.

The authorised representative in the EEA is
Dorling Kindersley Verlag GmbH. Arnulfstr. 124,
80636 Munich, Germany

MIX
Paper | Supporting
responsible forestry
FSC™ C018179

This book was made with Forest
Stewardship Council™ certified
paper - one small step in DK's
commitment to a sustainable future.
**For more information go to
www.dk.com/our-green-pledge**